THE
HISTORY OF
EL SALVADOR

THE HISTORY OF EL SALVADOR

Christopher M. White

The Greenwood Histories of the Modern Nations
Frank W. Thackeray and John E. Findling, Series Editors

Greenwood Press
Westport, Connecticut • London

Library of Congress Cataloging-in-Publication Data

White, Christopher M., 1974–

The history of El Salvador / Christopher M. White.
   p. cm. — (The Greenwood histories of the modern nations, ISSN 1096–2905)
   Includes bibliographical references and index.
   ISBN 978–0–313–34928–7 (alk. paper)
   1. El Salvador—History.   I. Title.   II. Series.
   F1486.W46   2009
   972.84—dc22   2008030539

British Library Cataloguing in Publication Data is available.

Library of Congress Catalog Card Number: 2008030539
ISBN: 978–0–313–34928–7
ISSN: 1096–2905

First published in 2009

Greenwood Press, 88 Post Road West, Westport, CT 06881
An imprint of Greenwood Publishing Group, Inc.
www.greenwood.com

Printed in the United States of America

The paper used in this book complies with the
Permanent Paper Standard issued by the National
Information Standards Organization (Z39.48–1984).

10   9   8   7   6   5   4   3   2   1

For Rufina Amaya

Contents

Series Foreword

The *Greenwood Histories of the Modern Nations* series is intended to provide students and interested laypeople with up-to-date, concise, and analytical histories of many of the nations of the contemporary world. Not since the 1960s has there been a systematic attempt to publish a series of national histories, and as series advisors, we believe that this series will prove to be a valuable contribution to our understanding of other countries in our increasingly interdependent world.

Some 40 years ago, at the end of the 1960s, the cold war was an accepted reality of global politics. The process of decolonization was still in progress, the idea of a unified Europe with a single currency was unheard of, the United States was mired in a war in Vietnam, and the economic boom in Asia was still years in the future. Richard Nixon was president of the United States, Mao Tse-tung (not yet Mao Zedong) ruled China, Leonid Brezhnev guided the Soviet Union, and Harold Wilson was prime minister of the United Kingdom. Authoritarian dictators still controlled most of Latin America, the Middle East was reeling in the wake of the Six-Day War, and Shah Mohammad Reza Pahlavi was at the height of his power in Iran.

Since then, the Cold War has ended, the Soviet Union has vanished, leaving 16 independent republics in its wake, the advent of the computer age has radically transformed global communications, the rising demand for oil makes the Middle East still a dangerous flashpoint, and the rise of new economic powers like the People's Republic of China and India threatens to bring about a new world order. All of these developments have had a dramatic impact on the recent history of every nation of the world.

For this series, which was launched in 1998, we first selected nations whose political, economic, and socio-cultural affairs marked them as among the most important of our time. For each nation, we found an author who was recognized as a specialist in the history of that nation. These authors worked cooperatively with us and with Greenwood Press to produce volumes that reflected current research on their nations and that are interesting and informative to their readers. In the first decade of the series, more than 40 volumes were published, and as of 2008, some are moving into second editions.

The success of the series has encouraged us to broaden our scope to include additional nations, whose histories have had significant effects on their regions, if not on the entire world. In addition, geopolitical changes have elevated other nations into positions of greater importance in world affairs and, so, we have chosen to include them in this series as well. The importance of a series such as this cannot be underestimated. As a superpower whose influence is felt all over the world, the United States can claim a "special" relationship with almost every other nation. Yet many Americans know very little about the histories of nations with which the United States relates. How did they get to be the way they are? What kind of political systems have evolved there? What kind of influence do they have on their own regions? What are the dominant political, religious, and cultural forces that move their leaders? These and many other questions are answered in the volumes of this series.

The authors who contribute to this series write comprehensive histories of their nations, dating back, in some instances, to prehistoric times. Each of them, however, has devoted a significant portion of their book to events of the past 40 years because the modern era has contributed the most to contemporary issues that have an impact on U.S. policy. Authors make every effort to be as up-to-date as possible so that readers can benefit from discussion and analysis of recent events.

In addition to the historical narrative, each volume contains an introductory chapter giving an overview of that country's geography, political institutions, economic structure, and cultural attributes. This is meant to give readers a snapshot of the nation as it exists in the contemporary world. Each history also includes supplementary information following the narrative, which may include a timeline that represents a succinct chronology of the nation's historical evolution, biographical sketches of the nation's most important historical figures, and a glossary of important terms or concepts that are usually expressed in a foreign language. Finally, each author prepares a comprehensive bibliography for readers who wish to pursue the subject further.

Readers of these volumes will find them fascinating and well-written. More importantly, they will come away with a better understanding of the contemporary world and the nations that comprise it. As series advisors, we hope that this series will contribute to a heightened sense of global understanding as we move through the early years of the twenty-first century.

Frank W. Thackeray and John E. Findling

Preface

El Salvador = The Savior

God, Union, Liberty

—The Salvadoran National Motto

In my country, there is no more God.

—Salvadoran character from
Oliver Stone's film, *Salvador*

El Salvador: the Land that God Forgot

—Title of a speech by Central America specialist,
University of Kansas Professor Emeritus
Dr. Charley Stansifer

El Salvador holds a special place in Latin American history. Its national motto of "God, Union, Liberty" speaks volumes of the people's desires and of the problems they have faced since the days of the first Spanish arrivals in 1522. That is to say that the search for these three elements is of the utmost importance to all Salvadorans, but in such conflicting ways that it has led to endless problems. Salvadorans have desperately sought a course to stability and peace for nearly 500 years and though they have not suffered war in the past 15, even the post–civil war era has witnessed violence and desperation on a level most Latin American nations would never accept. The Salvadorans only accept it because they have to in light of their recent as well as long-term past.

My first encounter with the people of El Salvador was during my junior year of high school. The civil war that lasted from 1980 to 1992 was still raging and had compelled several million Central American refugees to flee, many hundreds of thousands of which ended up in the southern part of my home state of California. Salvadorans made up fully half of those refugees and many thousands of them lived in my hometown of San Jose, in northern California, which has a rich history of Hispanic settlement dating back to the late eighteenth century. I had just returned from a year in Mexico learning Spanish and becoming accustomed to Latin American culture, and because I spoke their language I became a tutor to a handful of Salvadorans with little knowledge of English. However, they knew everything about hardship, as I soon found out after hearing stories of fleeing the military and guerrilla forces that displaced over a million people and caused the deaths of tens of thousands. As I came to know more and more of them and I heard their harrowing stories about fleeing the land they loved, I found myself feeling overwhelmingly interested in and concerned for a place I had only come to know through its refugees.

Those Salvadorans became my close friends and my experiences with them taught me as much as I have learned in any book on the subject. Whether talking about life growing up in the Salvadoran countryside over a plate of *pupusas* (main Salvadoran dish containing thick corn tortillas stuffed with various ingredients, usually including cheese and chicken), or working with them on English or swimming lessons, or relaxing by the campfire, my interactions with Salvadorans living in San Jose only reinforced the notion that often through great fear and suffering comes with great perspective. That is to say that their experiences and perspectives as refugees influenced my perspective as an aspiring world citizen.

I would continue to meet Salvadorans in the United States as well as Americans who had visited there while I was in college and in the Marine Corps. In fact, my Marine Corps recruiter had spent time on a U.S. military mission training the Salvadoran military during the 1980s while serving as a Green Beret for the U.S. Army. His stories stood out as a typical view among many Americans at the time who saw the Nicaraguan leftist revolutionary government of the Sandinista National Liberation Front (FSLN or Sandinistas) as a communist threat that might spill over into El Salvador, and eventually, in their minds, the rest of the hemisphere. My recruiter spoke of how he used to take aim with his sniper rifle at American aid workers trying to help the victims of the military, dubbing them communist sympathizers. He viewed the military as the only legitimate side and all others as the enemy. Of course this was a markedly different perspective from my friends who had fled violence from the Salvadoran military, but his view still represents the perspective of many Salvadorans during the civil war that saw the insurgents as terrorists. While the United Nations Truth Commission report of 1993 explains that the vast majority of the atrocities were committed by the U.S.-backed military, the guerrillas are also to blame for unnecessary suffering.

My first opportunity to visit the country came in the summer of 2003. By then, I had come to know El Salvador in other ways such as through books and more Salvadoran friends. I was still a graduate student at the University of Kansas and I had gone through a list of books on El Salvador, including such great works as Mark Danner's *The Massacre at El Mozote*, Thomas P. Anderson's *Matanza*, Tommie Sue Montgomery's *Revolution in El Salvador*, Charles Clements's *Witness to War*, Manlio Argueta's *One Day of Life*, and Joan Didion's *Salvador*, as well as more generalized books related to El Salvador such as William LeoGrande's *Our Own Backyard*, Walter LaFeber's *Inevitable Revolutions*, and Tina Rosenberg's *Children of Cain*, and several more. All these books as well as the films *Salvador*, *Romero*, and *Men with Guns* (about an unnamed Central American country), added to my depth of understanding about El Salvador that had been developing since those first stories I'd heard firsthand from Salvadoran refugees in high school. While in the country, I found the human atmosphere strikingly intense on a level I had never seen before in my travels throughout Latin America. Despite the palpable sense of the recent turbulent past still haunting the present, there was also a great sense of hope after centuries of inequality, dictatorship, civil war, and the struggle between tradition and modernity.

As I was on a larger trip encompassing Guatemala, El Salvador, Nicaragua, and Costa Rica, I was able to contextualize my visit to El Salvador in contrast to the rest of the nations I visited. For example, although Guatemala and Nicaragua have experienced terrible civil wars in the past few decades, there is indeed something different about El Salvador's experience. It is a very compact country with a tremendous amount of people for its size, which means that the civil war affected nearly everyone in some way. Guatemala and Nicaragua are several times larger than El Salvador and even though their wars were absolutely horrific, their sizes meant that many people were completely unaffected by the wars simply due to their locations. For example, the tourism industry was still vibrant during the Guatemalan civil war from 1954 to 1997 while tourism was virtually unheard of in El Salvador during their civil war, and while it has grown since then, it pales by comparison to its neighbors. My most recent trip in March 2008 showed me that tourism is growing, if only slightly.

The point is not to compare the horrors of these countries, but instead to highlight how El Salvador stands out among the countries of this region. My personal sympathies with the people of El Salvador do not rest on political ideology. I believe that matters little because there are indeed many valid histories of its people. There is the history of oppression against the Pipil, Lenca, and Chortí communities by the Spanish and later the Salvadoran military. There is the history of inequality that has resulted from colonial and modern structures of export-led economics. There is the history of indigo, cotton, coffee, sugar, chocolate, and manufacturing, as well as several other industries. There is the history of concentrated elite privilege on a scale unknown throughout the rest of Latin America, where the power of the so-called 14 families stretches back to the nineteenth century at least. There is the history of leftist political agitation dating back to 1932 and ending in 1992. And then there is the history of the U.S. role in El Salvador that is seen by some as good and others as bad, which dates back to the nineteenth century. Regardless of these conflicting yet parallel histories, what matters to me is that the story of the smallest country in mainland Latin America, which simultaneously has endured great hardship while maintaining a vibrant culture and an optimistic outlook for the future, is told to readers far and wide, and especially to those who may have never given the place a first, let alone a second thought, despite their own nation's enormous role therein.

Timeline of Historical Events

10,000 B.C.–6,000 B.C.	First indigenous arrivals to Central America
6,000 B.C.–2,000 B.C.	Domestication of plants and animals in Central America
1,200 B.C.	First verifiable advanced human settlement in El Salvador at Chalchuapa
250 A.D.	Ilopango Volcano erupts in Zapotitlán Valley
600	The village of Cerén is buried by volcanic eruption in western El Salvador
1054	Pipil era begins in western El Salvador with the arrival of the Toltecs from Mexico
1492	Columbus discovers the Americas
1500	Brazil discovered by the Portuguese
	The Hapsburg era begins on the throne of Spain
1502	Columbus discovers the Gulf of Honduras
1508	Mainland Mexico discovered

1516–1556	Charles I reigns as King of Spain
1521	Conquest of Mexico by Hernán Cortez
1522	First attempted Spanish conquest of El Salvador fails due to Pipil resistance
1524	Spanish occupation of El Salvador begins, Pedro de Alvarado invades
1525	Gustavo de Alvarado founds San Salvador
1528	Pedro de Alvarado conquers the Pipil Indians in western El Salvador
1530	San Miguel founded
	Pedro de Alvarado conquers the Lenca Indians in eastern El Salvador
1537–1547	Anti-Spanish Indigenous rebellion launched from Higueres
1542	All of Central America under the Kingdom of Guatemala
	New Laws passed, forbidding unjust exploitation of Indians
1548	Alonso Lopez de Cerrato named president of the Audiencia of Guatemala
1551	Catholic monastic orders enter El Salvador to Christianize the Indians
1556–1598	Phillip II is king of Spain
1598–1621	Phillip III is king of Spain
1610–1630	First indigo boom
1621–1665	Phillip IV is king of Spain
1625	Slave riots in San Salvador
1665–1700	Charles II becomes king of Spain, the last of the Hapsburg Dynasty
1682	Pirates attack the delta of the Lempa River
1701–1746	Phillip V is king of Spain, beginning the Bourbon Era in Spain

1746–1759	Ferdinand VI reigns as king of Spain
1754	El Salvador indigo baron Juan Fermín de Aycinena arrives in Guatemala
1759	Charles III is king of Spain
1763	Economic reforms instituted by Crown *visitador* José de Galvez
1799	Pirates attack the port of Acajutla
1800	La Escuela de la República opens
1808	Ferdinand VII becomes king of Spain
	Napoleon deposes King Ferdinand VII in Spain
1811	José de Bustamante becomes president of the Audiencia of Guatemala
	Liberal revolt in El Salvador led by Father José Matías Delgado
1812	The liberal constitution of the Spanish Cortes de Cadiz is written
1818	Carlos de Urrutia Montoya y Matos becomes president of the Audiencia of Guatemala
1821	Gabino Gainza becomes the last president of the Audiencia of Guatemala
	Independence from Spain is declared with the approval of the Acts of Independence, and on September 15, the United Provinces of Central America (also known as the Federal Republic of Central America) is born
1822	El Salvador becomes a state within the United Provinces of Central America
	Mexico invades El Salvador soon after United Provinces President Gabino Gainza calls for Mexican annexation
1823	Mexico withdraws from Central America
1825	Salvadoran citizen Manuel José Arce named first president of the United Provinces
1826	Central American civil war between Honduras, Guatemala, Nicaragua, Costa Rica, and El Salvador begins

1828	Guatemalan invasion and occupation of El Salvador
1832–1833	Indian rebellion led by Anastasio Aquino
1838	El Salvador independent as a nation
1841	La Universidad de El Salvador is founded
1841–1842	Honduran citizen Juan Lindo becomes first president of independent El Salvador
1842	Civil war in Central America ends, with El Salvador suffering the highest human loss
1842–1844	Presidency of Juan José Guzmán
1844–1845	Presidency of Francisco Malespín
1846–1848	Presidency of Eugenio Aguilar
1848–1851	Presidency of Doroteo Vasconcelos
1851–1854	First and Second presidency of Francisco Dueñas
1854–1856	Presidency of Honduran born José María San Martín
1856–1858	Presidency of Rafael Campo
1858–1859	Presidency of Miguel Santín del Castillo
1859–1863	Presidency of Gerardo Barrios
1863	Guatemalan strongman Rafael Carrera (1839–1865) invades and occupies El Salvador's two biggest cities, Santa Ana and San Salvador
1863–1871	Third presidency of Francisco Dueñas
1871–1876	Presidency of Guatemalan born Mariscal Santiago Gonzalez
1872–1898	Five peasant uprisings in the Izalcos region
1876–1885	Presidency of Rafael Zaldívar
1881–1882	Federal laws eliminating collectively held lands
1885–1890	Presidency of Francisco Menendez
1886	New constitution approved, which lasted until 1939
1890–1894	Presidency of Carlos Ezeta
1894–1989	Presidency of Rafael Antonio Gutierrez

1898–1903	Presidency of Tomás Regalado
1903–1907	Presidency of Pedro José Escalón
1907–1911	Presidency of Fernando Figueroa
1911–1912	Presidency of Manuel Enrique Araujo
1912	Assassination of Manuel Enrique Araujo
1912–1919	Presidency of Carlos Melendez
1919–1923	Presidency of Jorge Melendez
1923–1927	Presidency of Alfonso Quiñonez Molina
1927–1931	Presidency of Pío Romero Bosque
1931	Presidency and overthrow of Arturo Araujo
	Return of Farabundo Martí from exile
1932	Execution of Farabundo Martí
	La Matanza in which Maximiliano Hernandez Martinez kills between 10,000 and 30,000 people
1932–1944	Dictatorship of Maximiliano Hernandez Martinez
1939	New constitution approved under Maximiliano Hernandez Martinez giving unprecedented dictatorial powers to the central government
1944	General strike and overthrow of Maximiliano Hernandez Martinez led by students and Salvadoran Democratic Action
1945–1948	Presidency of Salvador Castañeda Castro
1948	The so-called Revolution of 1948 ends with the overthrow of Salvador Castañeda Castro
1950	Constitution implementing social reforms
1950–1956	Presidency of Oscar Osorio
1956–1960	Presidency of José María Lemus
1960	Overthrow of José María Lemus
1960–1972	The so-called democratic era in Salvadoran politics due to the emergence of viable political parties in opposition to the dictatorships that had dominated through the military since 1932

1962	José Napoleón Duarte named head of the Christian Democratic Party (PDC)
1962–1967	Presidency of Julio Adalberto Rivera
1967–1972	Presidency of Fidel Sanchez Hernandez
1969	The Soccer War between Honduras and El Salvador
1970	Former Communist Party activist Salvador Cayetano Carpio creates first insurgent group, known as the Popular Liberation Forces (FPL)
1971	The People's Revolutionary Army (ERP) is formed. This group will become the largest and most significant of the five guerrilla groups that form the Farabundo Marti National Liberation Front (FMLN) in the 1980s.
1972	Fraudulent presidential election leads to a loss for José Napoleón Duarte, who is driven into exile
1972–1973	Military occupation of three campuses of the University of El Salvador
1972–1977	Presidency of Arturo Armando Molina
1975	The Anti-Communist Wars of Liberation Armed Forces (FALANGE) is created in El Salvador
	The Salvadoran Institute of Agrarian Transformation (ISTA) is created to help distribute land to poor peasants
	Famed Salvadoran poet and revolutionary Roque Dalton is executed by the ERP
1977	Catholic Priest Rutilio Grande assassinated
	Military massacre of up to 50 protestors at San Salvador's Plaza Libertad
1977–1979	Presidency of Carlos Humberto Romero
1979	The Nicaraguan revolutionaries of the Sandinista National Liberation Front (FSLN) overthrow the dictatorship of Anastasio Somoza Debayle
	Army officers overthrow Romero and established a reform-minded junta aimed at stemming the rise of

	guerrillas through law enforcement and social and land reform programs
1980	Agrarian Reform Law passed, Archbishop Oscar Arnulfo Romero assassinated, four church women assassinated, the FMLN is established, incorporating all five guerrilla groups (FPL, ERP, PRTC [Central American Revolutionary Workers' Party], PCS [Partido Comunista Salvadoreno], RN [Resistencia Nacional]) under one umbrella organization
1981–1989	Presidency of Ronald Reagan in the United States, thus beginning the era in which the United States accelerates its military and other aid to the Salvadoran government. The aid eventually reaches $1 million/day.
1981	The Massacre at El Mozote takes place in which 700–900 unarmed civilians are killed by the elite, U.S.-trained Atlacatl Battalion in Morazán province
	The Nationalist Republican Alliance (ARENA) is founded by Roberto D'Aubuisson, well-known head of the Mano Blanca (the death squads)
1982	U.S.-sponsored elections in El Salvador lead to ARENA's dominance of the Legislative Assembly, and PDC candidate Alvaro Magaña becomes president (1982–1984)
1983	Barracks revolt in Cabañas led by Lt. Col. Sigfrido Ochoa, a new constitution is approved, the pope visits El Salvador, and the first effort at a peace accord began on Contadora Island, Panama.
1984	First internal effort at peace is initiated by President Duarte, who meets with guerrilla representatives in the mountain town of La Palma, which ends in failure.
1984–1989	Presidency of José Napoleón Duarte, even though the military dominates a large part of the government, particularly the war
1987	Costa Rican president and Nobel Peace Prize laureate Oscar Arias leads the Escipulas peace process in Guatemala
1989	Six Jesuits killed, ARENA candidate Alfredo Cristiani elected (1989–1994)

	Major nationwide FMLN offensive against the military signals the continued strength of the guerrillas, forcing the government to the bargaining table
	Maryknoll priest Father Roy Bourgeois begins School of the Americas Watch (SOAW) outside the gates of Fort Benning, Georgia after the murder of the six Jesuits
1989–1993	U.S. presidency of George H. W. Bush
1990	President Duarte dies of cancer after finishing his term
1992	National Commission for the Consolidation of Peace (COPAZ) Peace Accords signed in Mexico City, officially ending the civil war
1993	UN Truth Commission titled "From Madness to Hope: The 12-Year War in El Salvador: Report of the Commission on the Truth for El Salvador" is released, amnesty is given to most perpetrators of the violence by President Cristiani, the army is reduced by 50 percent, forcible retirement for officer class known as the *tondona* for their role in the civil war's human rights abuses
1994	ARENA candidate Armando Calderon Sol elected president (1994–1999), new National Civilian Police force created
1997	Neither of the two dominant parties has a majority in the legislative elections
1998	Hurricane Mitch hits, devastating Honduras and Nicaragua, while causing comparatively moderate damage to El Salvador
1999–2004	Presidency of ARENA candidate Francisco Flores
2001	Earthquakes, drought devastate economy
2003	President Flores sends Salvadoran troops to Iraq, against the wishes of the majority of the population
2004	Antonio Elías Saca elected
2007	Polls see FMLN ahead of ARENA

1

El Salvador Today

GEOGRAPHY

The Republic of El Salvador is the smallest, most densely populated country on mainland Latin America. It is in the middle of Central America, a region encompassing six other countries: Guatemala, Honduras, Belize, Nicaragua, Costa Rica, and Panama. There are seven million Salvadorans and this exacerbates poverty and environmental degradation. However, population density (824 per square mile) cannot explain El Salvador's problems. Massachusetts has 810 per square mile with a comparable population but with a per capita income 11 times that of El Salvador ($52,000 vs. $4,900). Why the difference? To name a few: El Salvador is a developing country with a history of inequality and oppression, and its formidable geography includes over 20 volcanoes in its southern mountain range alone in the midst of a hot, tropical environment. It also has an abundance of overstressed soil coupled with a high population density that increases its hardships.

El Salvador should be considered a microcosm for the issues surrounding Latin America and Central America for several important reasons. First, like the area from Mexico to Chile (mainland Latin America), El Salvador has a history of indigenous traditions that have been marginalized as a result of

GUATEMALA

HONDURAS

Chalatenango

Santa Ana

Ahuachapán

Sensuntepeque

Sonsonate

Nueva San
Salvador

⊛ **SAN SALVADOR**

Acajutla

San Vicente

La Libertad

San Miguel

La Unión
Puerto Cutuco

Puerto El Triunfo

*Golfo
de
Fonseca*

North Pacific Ocean

NICARAGUA

0   15   30 km

0   15   30 mi

Courtesy of Bookcomp, Inc.

Spanish conquest and colonization and the dominance of non-Indian groups for five centuries. Second, Central America was the most tumultuous Latin American region of the Cold War, as competing armed factions left especially Guatemala, Nicaragua, and El Salvador under siege, leaving 400,000 dead and millions more displaced. Third, El Salvador's geography has made conflict with its neighbors much more likely. The historical animosity between Hondurans and Salvadorans over border territory claimed by each side led to war in 1969 as the result of a Honduran land reform program that hurt Salvadoran immigrants. In addition, wars broke out between El Salvador and its neighbors several times in the nineteenth century over the future of Central American politics. There are many other examples worthy of mention here that will be elucidated later in the book. Needless to say, location as a geographical determinant of Salvadoran history has worked largely against the small nation.

But there is much more to El Salvador than war, and the specifics of its geography, when coupled with the activities of its people makes for an interesting human story. With a total area of 8,124 square miles, its dimensions paint the picture of a small, weak country. For example, El Salvador's 340 miles of border length are limited to a Pacific coastline and this fact puts El Salvador at a disadvantage against its northern neighbors of Guatemala and Honduras, who each share 200 miles and 136 miles of border with El Salvador, respectively. The nation's 190 miles of coast represent a very narrow portion of the country, but it is one of El Salvador's inviting features with sandy beaches that are home to Salvadoran and foreign beach dwellers alike and a vibrant international surfing community. Its territorial maritime claims extend 12 nautical miles from the shore, but El Salvador has an exclusive economic zone out to 200 nautical miles into the Pacific Ocean. The shrimping industry is particularly important to El Salvador in this regard, and this has led to environmental problems associated with excessive harvesting of the seas, which in turn has led to a reduction in overall sea life, water pollution, and other problems that place El Salvador within a much wider spectrum of difficulties that play a part in the global market for goods and services. Thus, its place in the world appears more and more significant.

El Salvador's jungle terrain is complemented by sandy beaches and volcanoes that rise thousands of feet overlooking bustling cities and tiny towns. As a tropical country, El Salvador's climate can be broken down into two seasons, each of which are completely unlike the seasons experienced in the United States, for example. The Salvadorans refer to the first season as winter, and it runs from May to October. This is the wet season, when the rains come every afternoon like clockwork. The rains are so powerful at times that travel halts entirely. Roads are often closed due to landslides, making it impossible for traveling. The country is especially green during this period in spite of the vast amount of deforestation that has occurred there. Less than one percent of the land is under any kind of protection, but there are several important protected areas, such as Montecristo National Park, El Imposible National Park, Cerro Verde, Deininger Park, and El Jocotal Lagoon. Yet, El Salvador has a long history of ecological difficulties that lead straight up to the present day, perhaps unlike the rest of Central America if we listen to specialist Howard E. Daugherty:

> The original vegetation of El Salvador has been almost totally destroyed as a consequence of a long period of human occupance and activity. Agricultural pursuits, the use of fire, the demands for fuel and construction timbers, and the need for pasture lands have taken a heavy toll on the original forests. The only remaining natural formations are the remnants of cloud forests in the northwest and mangrove forests along portions of the coast. But even these forests are steadily being attacked by agriculturalists and firewood gatherers and, in the case of the mangroves, by salt makers. It is only a matter of years (not decades) before the entire landscape of El Salvador will be a culturally induced phenomenon.
>
> The vegetation of El Salvador had been greatly altered through human agency before 1800 and nearly destroyed before 1900—before any major botanical research had been undertaken. Thus, the precise nature and distribution of the undisturbed formations are unknown.[1]

Today, Montecristo is the location of the country's only cloud forest.

The importance of maintaining the integrity of the land and its relationship with the weather can not be overstated when considering their support for agriculture. The Salvadorans refer to the second season as summer, and it is considered the dry season, lasting from November to April. El Salvador's principal agricultural exports of coffee, sugar, rice, corn, beans, oilseed, cotton, and sorghum all revolve around this seasonal cycle. Fully 19 percent of the nation's employment is dedicated to agricultural production, and therefore a large population depends on a steady ebb and flow of the weather. By comparison, the percentage of U.S. employment dedicated to farming, forestry, and fishing combined reaches less than one percent. This is but one of the significant economic indicators dividing the developing world from the developed world as one consistently finds much higher levels of labor forces in the former involved in agriculture, whereas the latter have much higher rates of industry, manufacturing, and other skilled jobs.

Even when studying only a few facts about the economics of El Salvador, it should become obvious just how important geography is to understanding this nation's history. Seemingly surface-level facts such as the weather or coastline length have tremendous implications for people when linked to a nation's economy, which in turn plays an integral role in everyone's life, and this increasingly means the lives of those doing business with El Salvador from outside its limited borders, such as Americans.

Aside from the two main seasons that control agricultural production, El Salvador's mostly mountainous terrain provides a temperate zone that dots the country's landscape. The central plateau is also a prominent feature when contrasted with the numerous peaks of varying heights. Its volcanoes spread across the south and the north, towering over many large and small cities down below. The nation's tallest volcano is the Volcan de Santa Ana (7,812 feet) and another prominent volcano is the Volcan Izalco (6,396 feet). Although not a volcano, El Salvador's tallest peak of Cerro El Pital rests within the northern mountain range of the Sierra Madre and stands nearly 9,000 feet above sea level. The southern mountain range is actually less continuous than the north as it is composed primarily of volcanoes. El Salvador is also the only Central American nation without a Caribbean coastline, limited as it is to the Pacific. This makes overland water transit difficult unless traveling via the Rio Lempa, El Salvador's longest river at 200 miles, and the only navigable one, which flows north from Honduras to the south through El Salvador and to the Pacific. Its largest lake is Lago Ilopango, which is 25 square miles, and lies east of San Salvador.

Being small often spells disadvantage in the developing world but it can sometimes have its advantages. Due to its location on the opposite side of the isthmus from the Caribbean, hurricanes affect El Salvador less than the rest of Central America. This is not always the case, as we saw with Hurricane Mitch in 1998, but Mitch devastated the Caribbean coast much more so as there were billions in damages and thousands of lost lives in Nicaragua and Honduras.

However, El Salvador's size can not prevent it from geographical factors beyond its control, and seismic activity is one of those factors. As a nation sitting within the zone known as the Pacific Ring of Fire that surrounds the Pacific Ocean Basin for 25,000 miles, causing high levels of seismic activity leading to earthquakes, tsunamis, and volcanic eruptions, Salvadoran earthquakes are legendary. It suffers from tectonic pressure from the Pacific Plate, the Nazca Plate, and the Cocos Plate, which when combined cause unforeseen disasters that weaken El Salvador's already debilitated social and economic structures.

Earthquakes have been a major problem throughout Salvadoran history. Most recently, a series of two earthquakes on January 13 and February 13, 2001 hit 7.6 and 6.6 on the Richter scale respectively, and killed over 1,000 people. The main problem of these quakes was a landslide that killed over 800 people. The landslides resulted not only from the earthquake but also from heavy deforestation that has plagued the country during the last century due to excessive coffee production and high population density. In the last century alone, 13 major quakes have wreaked havoc in this small country with the worst three occurring in 1951, 1965, and 1986. Not only is the seismic activity responsible for the high levels of devastation from the earthquakes, but the land's history of earthquakes has geologically weakened the plates supporting it, making it more and more vulnerable to damaging quakes in the future. In addition, soil erosion from agricultural practices and population density that stresses the soil increases the potential for these types of landslides, much like what we see in Haiti.

Diseases also increase after each quake because people are displaced and therefore more exposed to pathogens borne in untreated water. The lack of adequate health facilities and governmental assistance are other reasons why these disasters have a much bigger impact on developing countries like El Salvador. The damage to the Salvadoran health services infrastructure, food and water supplies, and its transportation were all exacerbated by the already impoverished status of the country, and this problem will not go away by itself. Volcanic activity also threatens the population at times, such as was the case on October 1, 2005, when the Ilamatepec Volcano spewed smoke into the air for several days and killed two people.

Another Salvadoran challenge is the extreme weather. El Salvador's position on the Pacific Coast leaves it vulnerable to extreme variations of wet and dry weather that El Niño and La Niña events make worse, leading to floods and droughts. The latest severe drought from the summer of 2001 destroyed 80 percent of the nation's crops and in a country as economically dependent on agricultural production for export and internal consumption, this further eroded El Salvador's infrastructure. By comparison, the California drought of 2006 that caused massive losses in that state's agricultural production did not lead to the same set of problems experienced by El Salvador. Whereas *livelihoods* were threatened after the California drought, *lives* were threatened and indeed lost in the Salvadoran drought. The difference is crucial in our comprehension of El Salvador as a nation with an alternate group of dilemmas faced by its population.

DEPARTMENTS

Similar to the United States, El Salvador is broken up into small governing regions. Its 14 departments include the prominent places of San Salvador (which includes the nation's capital), Santa Ana (which includes the second largest city), San Miguel (which includes the third largest city), and Morazán (the region most affected by the civil war of the 1980s), to name a few. A brief description of each follows.

Ahuachapán

Ahuachapán is El Salvador's westernmost department with its capital of the same name. It contains the Rio Paz, which is on the Guatemala-El

Salvador border as well as the Apenca-Ilamatepec mountain range with the Cerro Grande de Apaneca mountain. It has a population of 360,000, and it was the scene of the first battle between Salvadorans fighting against Mexican Emperor Agustin de Iturbide in 1822. Its economy depends on coffee, sugar, beans, and fruit.

Cabañas

This department is located in the center northern part of El Salvador with Sensuntepeque as its capital. The entire department is covered in hills rather than mountains, and the name of the department signifies "400 hills." As a department with one of the coolest year-round temperatures, it is attractive to tourists. It is also well known for the Cerro Pelón, as well as its bean and sugar cane production, and it has approximately 200,000 inhabitants.

Chalatenango

This department is in the northwest of El Salvador with its capital the same name as the department. Chalatenango is known for its Las Matras Archeological Ruins that contain remnants of ancient Mesoamericans, as well as the "5th of November" Hydroelectric Dam, and for having the nation's tallest peak, El Pital.

Cuscatlán

At the center of El Salvador, this department has the smallest area while having over 200,000 inhabitants. Cuscatlán is well known as the name of the initial western Salvadoran indigenous population. Suchichoto is one of its well-known towns, and although it used to be the capital of the department, it is now Cojutepeque, which is known for its chorizo. This region is filled with mountains and valleys.

La Libertad

Especially famous for its beaches within an hour drive of San Salvador, this southwest department has over 780,000 people and is a favorite of tourists seeking to ride the famous waves of El Salvador. The capital is Santa Tecla and the beach city of La Libertad is the setting of much of Oliver Stone's movie, *Salvador.*

La Paz

Located in the center south of El Salvador, its capital is Zacatecoluca and it has a population of over 300,000. Like Chalatenango, La Paz is known for its prehistoric remains such as rock writings. This is also the birthplace of the independence hero, Dr. Jose Simeon Cañas y Villacorta (1767–1838).

La Unión

This department has the easternmost city of El Salvador, La Unión, which is also its capital. It has a population of 300,000 and is known for its Conchagua Temple and its ancient ruins in Intipuca and Meanguera.

Morazán

Especially known as the zone most affected by the fighting during the civil war, Morazán sits on the northeast border with Honduras and is home to several important sites that will be mentioned in more detail later in the book. For example, the town of Perquín, in the northernmost part of the department, was the rebel stronghold of the Farabundo Marti National Liberation Front (FMLN) guerrillas throughout the war and remains a solid base of political support for the FMLN party today. The massacre site of El Mozote is also in Morazán, approximately 5 miles from Perquín. This massacre will be covered in detail later in the book. The department's population of 200,000 is sparsely spread across its numerous hills, valleys, and dense jungles, and its capital is San Francisco Gotera.

San Miguel

This eastern department is approximately two and one-half hours from the nation's capital by car. With a population of over 530,000, this department contains the nation's third largest city, San Miguel, which also serves as a hub for travel to many other parts of the country and the region.

San Salvador

The most important department, San Salvador is located in central west El Salvador. It contains the nation's capital, part of Lago Ilopango, and some of the most densely populated cities of the country, with over two million people. Although it is the center of political life, San Salvador was touched by the civil war in a surprisingly light manner by comparison to the countryside. It cultivates coffee, beans, and sugar, much like the rest of the western departments.

San Vicente

At the very center of El Salvador lies the department of San Vicente, with the capital by the same name. One of its claims to fame was San Vicente's position as the capital of the state of El Salvador when it was part of the Federal Republic of Central America. Its population today is over 230,000.

Santa Ana

As it is situated on the western side of El Salvador, Santa Ana had long-lasting ties to the Maya region of neighboring Honduras and Guatemala. The sites containing Maya artifacts are: The Trapiche, Casa Blanca, and Tazumal. The Chortí and Pokomam inhabited this area, and Chalchuapa was the main Maya city in this region. The Pipiles entered the zone of Santa Ana around 1200 to 1400 and they were eventually conquered by the Spanish conquistadors beginning in 1528. Its major volcanoes are Santa Ana, Chingo, and the Ilamatepec, and the Rio Lempa is also a mainstay of the department. Also important for tourism are the lakes of Guija and Coatepeque

Sonsonate

This department includes the integral railway that runs between San Salvador and the Pacific Coast port town of Acajutla in the south. With a population of 111,000, this department also contains the Sensunapán River and has a long history as a major producer of agriculture, manufacturing, pottery, cotton cloth, sugar, cigars, alcohol, starch, baskets, and mats for sale throughout Central America. As an important port, Acajutla has been involved in the export of coffee and sugar especially and the import of grains that spread throughout the country.

Usulután

One of the many places with a Náhuatl name (language originating in central Mexico), this southeastern department is also known for being in the region of the Lenca Indians, and its capital is the same as the department. It is also the largest department of the country and has over 350,000 people. The port of El Triunfo, Jiquilisco Bay, and perhaps the best beaches all can be found in Usulután.

SOCIETY

Some interesting comparisons can be made between El Salvador and the United States in terms of population. The U.S. population of just over 300 million is thus over 40 times the population of El Salvador and the U.S. median age is 36.6 compared to El Salvador, which is 22. Our population growth rates differ considerably as well, with El Salvador growing at a rate of 1.7 percent annually and the United States at only .9 percent. While the death rate in the United States (8.26/1,000 inhabitants) exceeds El Salvador (5.6/1,000 inhabitants), the net migration rate to the United States (3.05 migrants/1,000 inhabitants) is almost directly inverse to that of El Salvador (−3.54 migrants/1,000 inhabitants). This growing trend of Salvadorans leaving the country began in earnest as a result of the civil war of the 1980s that displaced fully one-fifth of its population. Half of them entered the United States and yet, the net growth rate in the Salvadoran population exceeds that of the United States by almost double.

These comparisons only make sense when understood within a proper context, much of which can be explained by the development standards in each country. Health indicators reveal even more about a country and infant mortality is a common way of identifying a nation's health situation. For instance, although the United States ranks relatively low in the developed world for infant mortality statistics, at 6.37/1,000 live births, it is still close to one-quarter the rate suffered in El Salvador (22.88/1,000 live births). However, life expectancy in El Salvador is close to 72 years, compared to 78 years in the United States. Another area in which our two nations are close is HIV/AIDS affliction among adults, with the difference only slight (United States with .6% and El Salvador with .7% of the population).

While not always considered a health statistic, education statistics also matter when considered alongside health standards. For example, the United States enjoys a 99 percent literacy rate compared to El Salvador's 80 percent rate, which matters considerably when we note the lack of educational opportunities of Salvadorans hoping to improve their access to better standards of living such as health care, potable water, and sanitized food. In fact, this is a great increase from the literacy rate of the 1980s, which was approximately 50 percent. What's more, literacy rates and school attendance between men and women give men a 5 percent advantage, which represents an aspect of the historically male-dominated social system characteristic of Latin America. This has typically given a strong institutionalized advantage that provides for a more secure economic, social, and political future for men over women in a country already divided by endless degrees of inequality.

Education is required for all citizens through grade 9, and public school is provided free of charge through grade 12. Despite this, one-half of the eligible children go to school and two-thirds of Salvadorans never finish the ninth grade. Due to their much higher quality, private schools are frequented at a much higher rate than public schools, giving a tremendous advantage to elite and middle class students over that of the majority poor living in the country.

There are several prestigious universities that attract students from across the region as well. The two main universities, La Universidad de El Salvador and La Universidad Centroamericana, each came under attack from the government forces during the civil war and are now recovering from these traumatic events. La Universidad de El Salvador, founded in 1841, was attacked and closed down by the military due to the national university's left wing presence. The second largest university, La Universidad Centroamericana, is Jesuit-run and was also the victim of attacks by the military. The most notorious of these witnessed the murder of six Jesuit priests, their housekeeper and her daughter, by the elite, U.S.-trained Atlacatl Battalion. Needless to say, university life in the United States has a much more docile history than in El Salvador, despite the minor yet obvious exceptions (such as Kent State in 1970).

While differences between the populations of El Salvador and the United States reveal a considerable amount, the internal differences within El Salvador unveil a history of struggle within a small territory. For example, the ethnic breakdown of 90 percent ladino (mixed white and Indian race), 9 percent Caucasian, and 1 percent Indian explains a lot about the past 500 years. Whereas Indians used to comprise fully 100 percent of the inhabitants for thousands of years while the Pipiles, Nahuas, Chortí and other native groups planted deep roots, their numbers have dwindled to the point of complete marginalization in the past century alone. Many factors went into this process, which eventually placed the dominant ladino and white populations above them. One possible reason for low census numbers of Indians is the potential for low claims of indigenous ancestry since the traumatic uprooting event called *La Matanza* in 1932, in which government forces hunted down Indians and dissident groups, killing up to 30,000 mostly unarmed people.

There are also many other unexpected ethnic groups that have played a role in national life in the past century in particular. Palestinians, Chinese, and Jewish groups of various faiths all include themselves in El Salvador's cultural landscape. In fact, the last presidential election (2004) witnessed an unprecedented phenomenon in which the two top contenders, Elias Antonio Saca Gonzalez (2004–present) and Schafik Handal were of Palestinian descent. The winner, Saca, is accompanied by the nation's first female vice president, Ana Vilma de Escobar.

As per the status quo among Latin American countries, the vast majority (83%) of Salvadorans are Roman Catholic. However, Rome's monopoly has been slowly eroding in the past century due to the influx of U.S.-trained Evangelical missionaries, whose word has spread throughout the region during this time. The Rockefeller-funded Oklahoma missionary school of the Summer Institute of Linguistics has contributed toward this general trend since the 1920s. Today, up to one million (one-seventh of the total population) Salvadorans are Protestant Evangelicals and represent a growing trend among all Latin American countries to slowly incorporate northern customs including free market capitalism, notions of governance, and religious practices.

Salvadoran culture is also quite representative of what one would find in much of the rest of Latin America. For example, fútbol (soccer) is the number one sport in El Salvador by far, with many levels of participation from the national team level to the local level, with large stadiums located in San Salvador, San Vicente, San Miguel, Santa Ana, and Zacatecoluca. Recently, however, such sports as surfing and auto racing have increased in popularity. There is also an interesting dichotomy of traditions in the European-indigenous contrasts that prevail in the country. The ancient Maya pyramids, indigenous regional names (Cuscatlán, Chalatenango, etc.) folk art, and ancient rock writings all represent the indigenous roots of El Salvador, while the colonial buildings, modern cities, art, language, and government all represent European influence. The mixture between them also led to the largest ethnic group of all, the ladino (or mestizo), which incorporates customs from both indigenous and European culture.

ECONOMY

El Salvador is in fact helping to set another trend in Latin America linked to its increasing involvement in the global capitalist market: dollarization. The incorporation of the U.S. dollar has been controversial in places such as Ecuador and El Salvador, but ever since 2001 the dollar has been the Salvadoran currency in an effort to stabilize the nation's economy. Economic indicators help spell out the real value of the Salvadoran economy. Its Gross Domestic Product (GDP) is 17 billion dollars with a real growth rate of 4.2 percent and a per capita income of 4,900 dollars. By comparison, the U.S. GDP is 13 trillion dollars; in other words, the U.S. economy is nearly 800 times as large as El Salvador's, while the U.S. population is only 40 times as large. But that does not signify a poor labor force in spirit, for the unemployment rate stands at only 6 percent in El Salvador, compared to 4.8 percent in the United States. This fact demonstrates a very active population that takes full advantage of its employment resources especially when considered in comparison to other Latin American countries. Countries with much stronger economies such as Argentina (10.2%), Costa Rica (6.6%), Chile (7.8%), and Uruguay (10.8%) all have higher unemployment rates than El Salvador. This of course also means that the average employed Salvadoran earns much less than their counterpart in the above countries, whose economies are much more diversified and who enjoy much higher levels of domestic and foreign investment, as well as tourism.

A significant indicator of how this fleshes out with the average Salvadoran is income distribution. While the unemployment rate is relatively low, its underemployment rate, while unknown officially, is high. We see this in the fact that 35.2 percent live below the poverty line, compared to 27.4 percent in Uruguay and 18.2 percent in Chile, for example. In addition, the lowest 10 percent of the population in El Salvador has 0.67 percent of the income while the highest 10 percent has 38.76 percent, but this trend is quite typical throughout the hemisphere. What is not typical in the region is the nature of El Salvador's income inequality. The country has a long history of being run by a highly concentrated elite class with an inordinate amount of power despite the nation's diminutive size as illustrated in this section of a 1980 *Foreign Affairs* article explaining the phenomenon of El Salvador's infamous "Fourteen Families":

El Salvador is burdened with the most rigid class structure and worst income inequality in all of Latin America. For over a century, the social and economic life of the nation has been dominated by a small landed elite known popularly as "the 14 families" (Los catorce), though their actual number is well over 14. The family clans comprising the oligarchy include only a few thousand people in this nation of nearly five million, but until recently they owned 60 percent of the farmland, the entire banking system, and most of the nation's industry. Among them, they received 50 percent of national income.[2]

The recent motion picture, *Innocent Voices* (2004), covers this issue well. The film shows how the Fourteen Families have been in control of El Salvador since the beginning of the Spanish presence there in 1524, and although their control has been much more gradual than the movie's depiction, it is commonly understood that their power has deep roots that have permeated throughout El Salvador's history as well as its fundamental institutions.

While the control of these families, which number in the hundreds in reality, has decreased in recent years, extreme inequality adversely affects the average Salvadoran. The small federal budget of only 2.82 billon dollars and a public debt of 42.6 percent of the GDP results in a weak infrastructure. The Salvadoran peasant or urban beggar has very little role in creating this federal budget or debt, yet these people increasingly suffer its consequences in the form of lost opportunities in employment and social services. Some of the roads are relatively unsafe as well (potholes and highway robberies are sometimes a problem), and schools, hospitals, and disaster services necessary for a highly functioning economy and society in general do not support the citizenry sufficiently. Energy consumption also presents a problem because El Salvador imports all of its petroleum and exports electricity and chemical products. Its economy is not diversified or robust enough to afford the importation and consumption of the energy levels necessary for growing the economy at a rate much higher than it is currently.

At the same time, its principal trading partners are the United States and Mexico, two strong economies with strong markets. El Salvador signed the Central American Free Trade Agreement (CAFTA) with the United States as well as Guatemala, Honduras, Nicaragua, Costa Rica, Panama, and the Dominican Republic in 2004, and they signed bilateral free trade agreements with Mexico, Panama, and the Dominican Republic. El Salvador also has 15 free trade zones that serve mostly the maquiladora industry that assembles clothing and other products for foreign consumption. Other measures toward free trade have been operating in El Salvador similarly to the liberalization processes common to much of the developing world since the 1980s. These include privatization of previously government-run industries such as banking, electricity, public pensions, and telecommunications, as well as the reduction of tariffs that impede international trade, much of which was implemented later than the rest of Latin America due to the civil war of the 1980s. In fact, the privatization initiatives were the work of President Alfredo Cristiani's (1989–1994) Stability Adjustment Programs (PAE) that sought to stabilize the nation's economy after 13 years of war devastated the country.

These alterations in the economy have had several results, some beneficial, some questionable. For example, inflation is low by comparison to the rest of the region at between three and 5 percent annually, and exports increased 19 percent from 2000 to 2006. However, imports increased more than 50 percent in the same period, raising the trade deficit to over 100 percent. And yet, the number one contributor to the country, remittances from the two million Salvadorans living abroad, makes up over 16 percent of the GDP. This has mixed consequences as well, since it raises prices internally. This is much less a problem for Salvadorans receiving these remittances than it is for the poor who lack these financial connections that would allow them to compete with their fellow Salvadorans with such connections. This also accelerates soil erosion and deforestation as home buyers purchase land in order to build houses outside the major cities.

TOURISM

Like the rest of Latin America, El Salvador has recently sought to increase its share of the tourism market that mostly caters to Westerners. However, due to the competition from neighboring Guatemala, Honduras, Belize, and Costa Rica, El Salvador remains a hidden gem. While still generating a record 1.7 billion combined dollars in the tourism industry between 1996 and 2006, its 7.1 million visitors spent less per capita than the average tourist in other countries in the region. Even the relatively isolated nation of Cuba received 1.9 million visitors in 2006 alone, but generated 2.1 billion dollars in revenues from them. The tourism infrastructure is still in the process of research and development, with efforts to harness the nation's cultural attributes in order to attract outsiders to the country. The lack of indigenous peoples in the country and the environmental degradation are major drawbacks to tourism, especially because the surrounding countries boast either strong indigenous attractions or ecotourism or both.

However, El Salvador has a comparative advantage in one area of the tourism industry: guerrilla tourism. Due to the heightened awareness of the civil war among Americans and Europeans, many people from these countries have been visiting El Salvador of late to go on guided tours of civil war zones in order to learn more about the nation's history. The federal government does not officially support these efforts to any significant degree, although it tacitly approves of any activity that brings more tourism to El Salvador.

Another tourist attraction is the Festival El Salvador del Mundo, which lasts from August 1st through August 5th every year as a testament to the Salvadoran dedication to the Roman Catholic Church. El Salvador del Mundo literally translates to "The Savior of the World" and this speaks volumes about the Salvadoran perception of the Church's role in their national life. The festival is biggest in San Salvador, where preparatory festivities begin several days in advance and last for a week afterward. Other important holidays include Semana Santa (Holy Week and Easter) in March and April, Independence Day on September 15, Día de la Raza (Columbus Day equivalent) on October 2, Day of the Dead on November 2, and of course, Christmas on December 25. While cultural events attract outsiders to El Salvador, it is true what many guidebooks say about the country's greatest attribute, its people. The people are genuinely family oriented and friendly. They are extremely proud of their resilience in the face of adversity that they have experienced since time immemorial.

What also appeals to outsiders who are lucky enough to know about it, is the Salvadoran cuisine. The main item of interest and enjoyment is the *pupusa. Pupusas* are made of thick, stuffed corn tortillas containing chicken and cheese and other ingredients. This well-known dish is rather simple to make and can be found in every city and town in El Salvador.

Crime is the biggest impediment to the tourism industry today. Crime statistics alone are bad enough, but the prevalence of firearms in El Salvador due to the 13 year civil war, as well as poverty and the continuous influx of Los Angeles-based street gang members known as the Maras Salvatruchas, also known as MS-13, has led to a culture that defines security through gun possession. The Maras only form part of the wider crime problem, however. Gun stores are abundant and men are often seen walking with an unconcealed weapon on the street. My hotel in San Miguel sat next to a gun store with the name "El Francotirador," which translates into "The Sniper" or "The Sharpshooter" and citizens are allowed to carry firearms in public, presumably for self defense. In recent years, robberies of tourists have increased, according to the State Department.

The history of the Maras is an example of the inescapable web connecting Central America and the United States. Beginning in 1972, Salvadoran immigrants formed gangs in Los Angeles to compete with rival American gangs. Their numbers swelled as thousands of undocumented Central Americans arrived in Los Angeles fleeing the civil war in the 1980s, leaving them in a precarious situation. The United States had a considerable role in their arrival here because the Carter, Reagan, and Bush Sr. administrations sent six billion dollars in aid to the Salvadoran government that caused the majority of the civilian deaths and displacements during the civil war.

The illegal status of the Salvadorans left many unemployed and many turned to street crime, drug trafficking, and human trafficking. The Maras that grew out of this are recognizable by their tattooed faces as well as bodies and the Federal Bureau of Investigation (FBI) has even created a special unit to deal specifically with them. The United States has recently captured and repatriated hundreds of Maras back to El Salvador, filling prisons to capacity with these former American gang members that were created as a result of the tumultuous events connecting the United States and Central America. Some estimates put their membership worldwide at 100,000.

The Maras and other criminals have also taken to assaulting El Salvador's roadways. As with much of Central America, El Salvador's poverty has limited travel options to underserviced and unprotected roads as well as relatively few airports, while providing a vibrant public transportation system at inexpensive prices. There are only four airports with paved runways in the country, with 71 airports without such accommodations. Railroads were in use until 2005 when they were shut down due to competition from other sectors, but with only 350 miles of track compared to 6,800 miles of road, even though 5,000 miles of those are unpaved, motor vehicles have taken over as the only form of ground transportation. This proportion of paved versus unpaved roads is not uncommon in Central America, however. By comparison, only one-fourth of Costa Rica's roads are paved, whereas the proportion is one-fifth in El Salvador.

GOVERNMENT

The Salvadoran government has been working to rectify many of these problems ever since the 1992 peace agreement was signed between the U.S.-backed government and leftist rebels led by the FMLN. Certain stipulations to accommodate combatants have been implemented in order to smooth the transition toward peace. However, the war also produced lasting effects that will take much longer to disappear. For example, the two warring factions now form the base of the two major political parties in El Salvador. The right-wing sector of the government during the 1980s fell under the Nationalist Republican Alliance Party (ARENA), which was founded in 1981 by death squad leader Colonel Roberto D'Aubuisson. D'Aubuisson, a former trainee of the U.S. Army School of the Americas in the Panama Canal Zone, formed ARENA in an effort to depose the ruling military junta at the time. ARENA has held the presidency since 1989 and currently holds only a slight lead (34 out of 84 seats) in the unicameral Legislative Assembly, with the left-wing FMLN party trailing closely behind with 32 seats. The current president, Elias Antonio Saca Gonzalez is a former media baron and a longtime ARENA party member.

The FMLN also has its roots in the civil war. Although it has not won a presidential election, it does hold enough political influence to make opponents nervous. These include ARENA and the U.S. government that has openly supported ARENA since 1989. The FMLN began officially in 1980 as an umbrella organization uniting four guerrilla factions along with the Communist Party of El Salvador in order to oppose the government forces that had killed over 10,000 civilians in the three prior years. The group takes their name from the leftist insurgent leader Farabundo Marti, who was executed in 1932 by the government of Maximiliano Hernandez Martinez. In 1932, Hernandez Martinez unleashed death squads onto the countryside that massacred up to 30,000 people. The martyrdom of Marti as well as the repression against the population from the dictatorship left an imprint on Salvadoran society that has lasted until this day. However, Salvadorans also remember the FMLN bomb attacks and kidnappings of the 1980s. This memory hurts its chances of winning the presidency. At the same time, many associate the right-wing ARENA with the death squads that terrorized the population on a level that far surpassed the guerrilla atrocities.

NONGOVERNMENTAL CONNECTIONS TO THE UNITED STATES: SISTER CITIES

The civil war in El Salvador caused a great outpouring of concern from American citizens operating outside of the government. There were thousands of cases of Salvadoran refugees hosted by Americans working through human rights organizations with connections to El Salvador. Thousands of Americans risked their lives to provide aid and relief to the war-torn nation, and some even lost limbs or even their lives doing so. One of the added effects of these activities is the lasting connections between our two peoples. A recent story in the American press illustrates this well. In 1987, citizens from Cambridge, Massachusetts visited the village of San Jose las Flores in El Salvador to speak with Salvadorans affected by the war. Their stories touched the visitors so much that they have sent aid to help the fledgling town of 300 survivors recover ever since then. Today, San Jose las Flores, through support from their sister city, has 4,000 people and is growing stronger. In another case, Kenneth Cott, professor emeritus of Latin American history at Washburn University, has been leading groups of people from the Trinity Presbyterian Church in Topeka, Kansas, for 15 years now to the small town of Talpetates in the central part of the country. They have provided school and medical supplies throughout this period and have established connections that stretch across the continent.

And these types of stories have been duplicated across El Salvador in communities touched by Americans who were touched by the humanity of the Salvadorans. The story of these people follows within these pages, and it is my hope that readers will not only see this as a general history of the smallest country in Latin America, but as a story of a people that have never stopped struggling for the same dreams and aspirations most readers would not dream to live without.

NOTES

1. Howard Edward Daugherty, "Man-Induced Ecological Change in El Salvador," PhD Dissertation, Univ. of California–Los Angeles, 1969, 42–43, quoted in William R. Fowler, Jr., *The Cultural Evolution of Ancient Nahua Civilizations: The Pipil-Nicarao of Central America* (Norman: University of Oklahoma Press, 1989), 81.

2. William LeoGrande and Carla Anne Robbins, "Oligarchs and Officers: The Crisis in El Salvador," In *Foreign Affairs,* Summer 1980.

2

Pre-Columbian El Salvador

El Salvador does not stand out in pre-Columbian history by comparison to regions such as the Central Valley of Mexico, the lowlands of Guatemala, the Yucatan, or the Central Andes of South America. It nevertheless contributed to indigenous America prior to and since the arrival of Europeans. The history of Salvadoran Indians in the five centuries since the conquest also represents one of the most intense cases of loss and displacement witnessed in all of Latin America, namely because it continued into the twentieth century, leading to their virtual elimination. The history of pre-Columbian El Salvador can be broken down into the following periods: The Lithic, Archaic, Early Pre-Classic, Middle Pre-Classic, Late Pre-Classic, Classic, Post-Classic, and the conquest. This chapter will cover the most significant aspects of each of these periods and will also go into detail about the dominant indigenous group, the Pipil.

THE LITHIC PERIOD

The Indians of El Salvador have been participating in much larger phenomena of their region throughout history. They had a strong role to play in the spread of culture and civilization that began in the Americas with arrivals from the north who had crossed the Bering Land Bridge approximately 13,000 years ago. People began arriving in Central America some time within the Lithic Period that covers 10,000 B.C. to 6,000 B.C. During this time, bands of hunter-gatherers planted roots in *Mesoamerica,* the region including central and southern Mexico, the Yucatan, and northern Central America. One of the strongest sources of evidence attesting to this is the cultivation of maize beginning in southern Mexico in approximately 5,000 B.C. and it spread throughout Mesoamerica quickly thereafter. This was merely 1,000 years after wheat and barley were first cultivated in the Fertile Crescent of the Middle East, the first such place to create sedentary agriculture. While maize and other crops made their way to El Salvador, the new arrivals probably had a harsh first few centuries. If estimates are correct, the Coatepeque Volcano in western El Salvador erupted 10,000 years ago, close to the time of the first settlers. Salvadoran volcanic activity has plagued its history ever since and the inhabitants who remained to plant physical and cultural roots quickly grew accustomed to mobility in the face of this danger.

THE ARCHAIC PERIOD

A major shift in Salvadoran Indian history took place between 6,000 and 2,000 B.C. with the widespread domestication of animals and plants. This led to the establishment of sedentary agriculture and as a result, permanent settlements and the eventual rise of civilization in El Salvador. The cultivation of maize in particular had a tremendous impact due to its high caloric yield per acre when compared to the cereal grains of Europe and this food became the mainstay for Salvadoran Indians. However, maize was more important in the highlands by contrast to the lowlands and coastal areas where its growth was not as easy. As a result, trade in highland products such as maize and lowland products such as seafood and seashells developed between these locations. Beans and squash joined the equation to form the holy trinity of the Mesoamerican diet of maize, beans, and squash, all of which possess nutrients that complement one another when consumed together. This period also witnessed the entrance into El Salvador of Mayan-rooted dialects, probably as early as the third millennium B.C. and these languages spread north as far as Yucatan, Guatemala, and Chiapas (southern Mexico), as well as south to El Salvador. However, there were still no large urban areas, and thus neither were there pyramids, hieroglyphics, organized labor, imperialism, or any of the other accoutrements of advanced civilization. The difference between the Archaic Period and those that follow is this set of essential elements of advancement. By contrast, ancient Mesopotamia had established its first urban area in Sumer by 4,000 B.C. and coastal Peru had at least one concentration of 30 urban areas by 3,000 B.C.

However, the Salvadorans were on the frontier of civilization due to their location 500 miles south of where the first advanced Mesoamerican culture (the Olmecs) originated and 3,000 overland miles north of Peru. These distances even today are difficult to travel through due to the mountainous and tropical jungle terrain that covers almost the entire area. The jungle even acts as a buffer zone within Mesoamerica today where torrential downpours, landslides, volcanic eruptions, earthquakes, scorching hot and humid weather, as well as stinging insects make the journey difficult even with modern transportation. To the south, there are hundreds of miles of jungle through which no vehicle can travel to this day between Panama and Colombia, and this natural impediment to overland mobility would have inhibited communications and thus political, cultural, and trade relations between El Salvador and the Andes region. Therefore, the Salvadoran Indians were largely isolated geographically and thus had to depend on themselves as well as the creation and maintenance of networks to the north and south for their advancement in future years.

THE EARLY PRE-CLASSIC PERIOD

Beginning around 2000 B.C. and ending in 1000 B.C., the chronological record becomes much clearer because Salvadoran Indians started leaving behind more tangible cultural evidence. 1200 B.C. was the earliest verifiable date of an excavated human settlement in El Salvador. The western ruins at Chalchuapa represent the longest inhabited urban area (over 2,500 years) in the country and show an abundance of artifacts that demonstrate El Salvador's role in Mesoamerican civilization. Located in the Zapotitán Valley, Chalchuapa rests on the southeast frontier of the future realm known as the Maya world. At an altitude of 2,300 feet, Chalchuapa is near the Rio Paz and occupies almost two square miles with its 66 foot high central pyramid, its 58 large mounds, and 87 platforms that were used as house foundations. The two nearby ancient volcanoes at Laguna Cuzcachapa and Laguna Seca have archeological remains that show their extensive ritual significance for the Chalchuapans, as has been common for Indians across the Americas who view volcanoes, mountains, lakes, rivers, and other natural phenomena as possessing great spiritual significance.

What makes Chalchuapa stand out within El Salvador at the time was their creation of an organized society within an urban framework. This signified a central authority, religious organization, labor units for construction, urban planning (albeit rudimentary), organized agricultural production, controlled trade networks, and specialized cultural and trade crafts. The rest of El Salvador would follow in the footsteps of both Chalchuapa and outsiders mostly descending from the north, such as the Olmecs and the Maya.

THE MIDDLE PRE-CLASSIC PERIOD

This Middle Pre-Classic period (1000 B.C.–400 B.C.) witnessed the entrance of the fathers of Mesoamerican civilization known as the Olmecs. This emerging culture rooted in southern Mexico brought several cultural attributes to El Salvador that helped to bring the territory into the newly surging civilizations developing to the north that would eventually stand out as among the most advanced in the world at the time. This period of Mesoamerican civilization was dominated by this ever-expanding empire whose bases were far to the north of El Salvador, near the Gulf Coast of Mexico. The Olmecs are best known for their colossal stone heads, as well as the creation of many thriving cities with pyramids, mounds, and artistry, on a level far and above any of their contemporaries.

The Olmec cities sustained themselves through expansion of trade and conquest and evidence suggests that they arrived as far south as Chalchuapa in order to use the Salvadoran site as an outpost on the southeastern fringe of the empire. At over 500 miles from their centers of control in Mexico, the Olmecs would have been able to better control the obsidian trade from Ixtepeque, located in Guatemala just over the border with El Salvador. Another major site of Guatemala linking Chalchuapa to the Olmecs was Kaminaljuyu, which lies just 74 miles away and was important to Chalchuapa for its pottery and other trade items. This represented a chain extending from El Salvador to southern Mexico in which the Olmecs maintained dominance over trade reaching back to 1200 B.C. The Olmecs probably introduced such elements to the Chalchuapa region as the chipped stone industry and the Mixe-Zoque language. Chalchuapa's Monument 12 even has a rubbing deemed by archeologists to be Olmec in style dating back to this era.

Another western El Salvador site influenced by the Olmecs was Santa Leticia, situated in the highlands at 4,200 feet in elevation. A puzzling aspect of Santa Leticia is the large stone potbelly sculptures that clearly illustrate a connection to the Olmecs. Actual Olmec artifacts have also been found in the greater region of Ahuachapan in which Santa Leticia was located. These potbellied sculptures are less refined and a bit smaller than the colossal Olmec heads of Gulf Coast Mexico and they are also different by the fact that the Santa Leticia pieces depict entire bodies, not just the heads. Nonetheless, the similarities no doubt point to the extent of Olmec influence in El Salvador.

Settlement was denser along the Pacific coast of Central America due to its access to the seas for water travel, trade, and fishing, along with the highlands due to its more temperate climate. It was only logical that these higher population densities produced more advanced civilizations, and their connections to the Olmecs placed El Salvador within the future realm of one of the most advanced civilizations to grace the pre-Columbian landscape, the Maya.

THE LATE PRE-CLASSIC PERIOD

The Late Pre-Classic period in El Salvador encompasses 400 B.C. to 250 A.D. and witnesses the rise of the Maya, who replace the Olmec as the dominant culture in Mesoamerica. Chalchuapa began to expand its power and size as well, moving on its own away from Olmec dominance just as the Olmecs faded from the scene and the Maya surged in Guatemala, Honduras, Yucatan, and Chiapas. Other Salvadoran sites also begin to emerge during the Late Pre-Classic period such as El Trapiche, Cerro Zapote, Atiquizaya, Acajutla, Quelepa, and Santa Leticia. As Late Pre-Classic sites such as Chalchuapa grew, densely populated lowland centers drove many people to settle the highland towns such as Santa Leticia that had been occupied since 600 B.C. and with these migrations became much stronger.

The famous Classic Maya sites were already occupied during the Late Pre-Classic period. They were in the process of laying the groundwork for their later advancement that surpassed anything seen in the Americas to that point. Most notably, Tikal in Guatemala, Palenque in Chiapas, and Copan in Honduras would soon create magnificent structures such as towering pyramids of great artistic beauty, various forms of writing, and hieroglyphs, illustrating its nascent rise to glory that lasted until the ninth century. Meanwhile, western El Salvador's Zapotitán Valley suffered from a tragedy when the volcano Ilopango erupted in approximately 250 A.D. This eruption buried and preserved most of Chalchuapa and the surrounding areas. Archeological data show that the Chalchuapans had developed Maya-style hieroglyphics containing numeric and calendar symbols such as Monument 1's picture of a king holding a head while seated below rows of Maya symbols. While Ilopango devastated the main part of Chalchuapa, its southern region of Tazumal recovered by the end of the Classic Era (300 A.D.–900 A.D.) By the time of the Spanish arrival in the sixteenth century, the Tazumal/Chalchuapan language was Pokomam Maya, which gives us an idea as to how El Salvador was influenced by the Maya throughout its pre-Columbian history.

Overall, the Late Pre-Classic period should be understood as a much different situation for El Salvador than for the rest of Mesoamerica in two crucial ways. First, it was a time of very little advancement for those living in the western areas devastated by the eruption of Ilopango in 250 A.D. just as the northern Mesoamericans were on the march forward with little hindrances of this sort. Cities such as Teotihuacán, in fact, held 200,000 inhabitants at this time and had created the largest pyramids in the Americas. At the same time, the citizens of western El Salvador were mostly just seeking methods of survival in the aftermath of the disaster, and had little time for moving in tandem with the imperial designs cultivated by the Maya and Teotihuacanos. Second, those Salvadorans less affected by the volcano were able to follow in the wake of the Classic Maya's acceleration of civilization. However, it should not be overlooked that Chalchuapa was well on its way down this path when the eruption stopped it in its tracks.

THE CLASSIC PERIOD

From 300 A.D. to 900 A.D., Mesoamerica as a whole thrived unlike it ever had. The city of Teotihuacán (100 B.C.–700 A.D.), located 28 miles northeast of Mexico City, developed into the largest city, with over 200,000 inhabitants. It dominated trade from its centralized location that enabled it to extend its influence throughout Mesoamerica in competition with the Maya to the south. The Maya dominated the southern portion of Mesoamerica, and both the Maya and the Teotihuacanos excelled in the creation of modern cities, architecture, war fighting, and writing.

El Salvador was heavily influenced by these cultures as we can see from numerous studies on the topic. The sites at Quelepa in the east and Chalchuapa in the west contain the typical Classic Maya characteristics such as the burial of family members under dwellings; the construction of mounds or platforms; ball courts; cardinal direction-oriented, square structures (pyramids, homes, etc.); cities that demonstrate a sense of community planning; and large square plazas. Both of these sites were occupied during the early stages of Maya development that also coincided with the rise and fall of the Olmec, which indicates how El Salvador was part of the larger development processes of the dominant Mesoamerican cultures of the time.

Great changes occurred in the third century A.D. for most Salvadoran Indians as the Maya influence that had penetrated El Salvador in the Late Pre-Classic era began to fall precipitously. This downfall had at least two causes related to the eruption of Ilopango around 250 A.D. First, volcanic ash made the surrounding area almost uninhabitable for up to two centuries afterward while the rest of the Maya region accelerated in leaps and bounds along with Teotihuacán. Secondly, massive rates of death and out-migration resulting from the omnipresent ash covering the ground in the vicinity of the volcano caused a dramatic and sudden loss of agricultural productivity and obliterated a crucial link in regional trade routes. Conversely, this reduced the market competition for those Maya living to the north in Guatemala, Honduras, and Chiapas, which must have bolstered their superiority in the region.

The Ilopango disaster most likely led to waves of migration north that introduced Salvadoran culture to the northern Maya. The unique Usulután pottery characteristics found throughout the Classic Maya realm of Guatemala are important in this regard as evidence suggests that the techniques originated in the southern Maya zone that included El Salvador. Other aspects such as the notion of kingship and its representation on pyramids and hieroglyphs in the

Classic Maya zone began shortly after the eruption at Ilopango. This could be a matter of coincidence to be sure, but some researchers have identified this occurrence as the possible result of migrations north out of El Salvador after the eruption.

An example of a Classic Maya site in El Salvador that revived itself for a short while after Ilopango is Cerén, which lies to the southeast of Chalchuapa and to the west of modern-day San Salvador. Similar to Chalchuapa, Cerén was also buried in ash but from an eruption by the Laguna Caldera in the middle Classic era, probably around 600 A.D. The Cerén site has evidence of highly skilled agriculture with rows for plant cultivation flanked by drainage areas located near homes. The Maya at Cerén most likely carried out swidden agriculture (slash and burn) and crop rotation for farming maize fields known as *milpas* and they maintained household gardens known as *solares* for growing personal use crops such as chilies, beans, squash, and other foods. They were also known to have used human waste as a fertilizer for manioc, maize, and other crops. Just like the famous volcanic burial of ancient Pompeii, the eruption near Cerén preserved the site in a dense layer (9 feet deep) of volcanic deposition. This indicates the possibility that several eruptions from one or more surrounding volcanoes occurred either simultaneously or over the course of many years. The highland Maya presence at Cerén is abundant with excavations of a single home containing pottery, weaving, stone tool production, food preservation containers and pantries, and a walkway that led to an outbuilding serving as a stone tool production facility.

One problem the Cerén inhabitants had faced on the eve of the Laguna Caldera eruption was the soil quality that had been depleted due to the Ilopango eruption just over three centuries before the site's demise. In fact, the entire Zapotitán Valley suffered this fate to varying degrees. Prior to the eruption, the Cerén had been under occupation at least since the Pre-Classic era and was abandoned after the Ilopango eruption for about 200 years. Thus, Cerén inhabitants had only recently returned to the site when the Laguna Caldera eruption drove them out. Although not a large city, it was certainly of medium size and importance in the Classic Maya realm as gleaned from the amount and quality of artifacts archeologists have uncovered at the site.

Quelepa, a Lenca city located 5 miles north of San Miguel, faced a completely different set of circumstances from Cerén. The Lenca had Maya roots but only maintained strong connections until the middle of the Classic period. Quelepa's history has been broken down into three major phases documenting its 1,500 year history. The Uapala phase (from possibly 500 B.C. to 150 A.D.) saw the introduction of urban planning and city expansion as leaders consolidated trade networks in ceramics and other items with its neighbors within El Salvador and Guatemala. The Shila phase (150 A.D.–625 A.D.) is characterized by its advanced architecture and terracing. What stands out here is the fact that the volcanic disasters experienced in western El Salvador in 250 A.D. and 600 A.D. did not affect Quelepa, which thrived. The Lepa phase (625 A.D.–1000 A.D.) coincides with the Late Classic to Early Post-Classic periods of Maya history, even as evidence suggests Quelepans avoided contact with western El Salvador and Guatemala while establishing connections to the Gulf Coast of Mexico. Archeologists found ceramic designs and other items from Veracruz that indicate an introduction of Gulf Coast Indians into the Lenca region in approximately 600 A.D. By 1000 A.D., much like its Classic Maya counterparts, Quelepa was abandoned for unknown reasons.

The end of the Classic period of the Maya came in the ninth century A.D. due to largely unknown reasons despite massive research into the subject. Most recently, Mel Gibson's major motion picture *Apacalypto* speculates about these causes. One important contributing factor toward this cataclysm is that the great city of Teotihuacán was abandoned after war broke out and a massive fire destroyed much of the city in the early eighth century. The aftermath of this event must have caused massive disruptions in trade and politics throughout Mesoamerica. Through analysis of hieroglyphs, archeologists have surmised that warfare took place between the dominant Maya cities of northern Central America and that nearly all inscriptions ended in the ninth century there. Researchers speculate that overpopulation, deforestation, warfare, disease, drought, and other problems plagued the Late Classic Period, which witnessed the abandonment of every major Classic Maya site. Salvadoran Indians in Santa Leticia and Tazumal lost important markets to the north with these disruptions while cities such as Cerén had long been reduced or abandoned by the end of this period. Salvadorans soon faced a new set of challenges entirely with the arrival of Toltec influence from the north that would eventually cause El Salvador to rise from the ashes.

THE POST-CLASSIC PERIOD

When the Spanish conquistadors arrived in El Salvador in the early sixteenth century, they noted that the language spoken by the Salvadoran Indians resembled the language of the Aztecs they had recently conquered. This occurred due to processes taking place throughout all of Mesoamerica during the Post-Classic period (1000 A.D.–1550 A.D.). A new imperialistic group known as the Toltec dominated the early part of this period from their capital at Tula, not far from the formerly great city of Teotihuacán. The downfall of Teotihuacán and the Classic Maya allowed for the Toltecs to fill in the power vacuum. This power spread from Tula through Puebla in the east then south to Oaxaca, then northeast through the Yucatan peninsula, and south through Central America. The Toltecs reached as far as El Salvador carrying their culture with them, as can be seen in the Pipil civilization that has lasted albeit marginally to this day.

However, unlike the changes that occurred in El Salvador during the Classic period, the changes taking place in the Post-Classic period expanded slowly for the average Salvadoran Indian who nonetheless still found themselves affected by larger processes shaping the entirety of Mesoamerica.

The tenth and eleventh centuries were times of recovery in the Maya region from the ninth century upheavals discussed above. The Toltecs, unlike the Classic Maya and the Teotihuacanos, were considered to be of a higher cultural pedigree than their predecessors. In fact, the Aztecs that ruled much of Mexico up to Hernán Cortez's conquest of the country in 1521 proudly asserted their Toltec ancestry as a means of legitimizing their reign over the region. The Toltec culture's most prominent feature came in the deity of the feathered serpent, known as Quetzalcóatl in central Mexico and western El Salvador, Ehecatl in eastern El Salvador, and Kukulcán in the Yucatan. There are great stone monuments to the feathered serpent across Mesoamerica, most notably in Teotihuacán, Tula, Chichén Itzá, and Tenochtitlán. The fact that Salvadoran religious lore fits in with these cities that embody the highest levels of Mesoamerican civilization explains a lot about the world Salvadoran Indians inhabited.

THE PIPIL ERA

The first scholar to synthesize the history of the Pipil migrations from the north in Mexico to the south in El Salvador was nineteenth century researcher Ephraim George Squier. His research was later followed up by other scholars over the course of the next century and a half. The Nahua migrations may have even begun as long ago as 500 A.D. in small numbers. However, the larger influx of Nahuas who in El Salvador were known as the Pipils resulted from Toltec influence at the end of the Classic period and continued into the peak years of the Post-Classic (1350 A.D.).

It is believed by many that the beginning of the Pipil era of dominance in El Salvador began in the year 1054 when a Toltec prince supposedly led the Pipils to conquer the local Maya known as the Chortí. The Chortí then moved north into the mountainous zones of Chalatenango, Tequechonchongo, and Chicongueza, among other places. The Pipil soon founded the prominent cities of Izalcos and Cuscatlán, which are still well known for their indigenous traditions today. The former Pipil territory of western El Salvador to the south and west of the Lempa River was known as Cuscatlán. For close to 500 years leading up to the arrival of the Spanish in the 1520s the Pipil territory extended over most of western and central El Salvador as well as some of Guatemala and Honduras and was broken into two or three governing zones. These were Cuscatlán, Izalcos (700–800 square miles each), and perhaps Nonualcos (400 square miles). Other groups of importance in El Salvador were the

Lenca, Matagalpa, Chortí, Pokomam, and Jinca. One prominent exception to Pipil dominance came toward the end of the Post-Classic period when the Pokomam conquered Chalchuapa and expelled the Pipil.

In comparison to the northern Maya region during the height of the Classic period, Salvadoran city structures were small under both the Maya and the Pipils. Their cities tended to have several thousand, with perhaps as many as 10,000 in Cuscatlán itself during the Post-Classic period. By comparison, this meant that at their height, Pipil cities had half the population of the dominant Mississippi Valley city of Cahokia, the largest pre-Columbian city north of the Rio Grande, also thriving during that era.

As evidence of the significance of El Salvador's indigenous past, Salvadorans take pride in referring to themselves as Cuscatlecos in reference to their Pipil roots. The term Cuscatlecos bares a strong similarity to many Mexican regional names inhabitants give themselves such as Chiapanecos (from Chiapas) or Tlaxcaltecas (from Tlaxcala, also an indigenous tribal name), and many other examples. Some well-known Pipil settlements as of 1524 were Acatepeque, Tacuba, Ataco, Atiquizaya, Ahuachapan, Apaneca, Juxutla, Acaxutla, Tonala, Tacuscalco, Nalingo, Masahúat, Juayua, Quetzalcoatitán, Chalchuapa, Ateo, Quetzaltepeque, Gueymoco, Coyo, Chilteupán, Zinacantán, Tequepa, Chinameca, Olocuilta, Guazapa, Coatepeque, Suchichoto, Xilopango, Montepeque, Cuxutepeque, Huiziltepeque, Zoquitlán, Tecoluca, Ixtepeque, Zacatecoluca, and Nonualco. It should be noted that most of these names would sound odd in Guatemala, while they fit right in with Mexico. For example, note the following Mexican place names: Tenochtitlan, Tlaxcala, Tehuacán, Tlaquepaque, Mazatlan, and Tlatelolco. On the other hand, Guatemala's entirely Maya background can be seen in all regions of that country, with place names such as Quetzaltenango, Panajachel, and Chichicastenango. However, the Nahua prominence established in El Salvador during the Post-Classic period meant that Mexican-sounding place names survived. The prevalence of many Nahua names to the east of the Lempa River such as Jiquililisco, Aguacayo, Ozatlán, and Usulután also suggest that the Pipil and the Lenca may have shared control over eastern El Salvador up through the time of the conquest.

This array of Mexican cultural attributes further explains El Salvador's integrated place within Mesoamerica as a whole, even if it stood on the frontier. Examples of this abound. The Nahuat spoken by the Pipils was close to the Náhuatl spoken by many Toltecs and most notably the Aztecs of central Mexico. The main difference between the two is that Nahuat drops the "l" quite common to Náhuatl, thus often eliminating the combined sound made by the "tl" when spoken together. Of course, there are exceptions, as can be seen in the name of Cuscatlán, which preserves the "tl" sound in the middle.

Cuscatlán also saw the introduction of Mexican cultural elements. For example, there are several *chac mools,* a type of statue depicting a reclined figure holding a bowl on its belly that is predominantly found across northern Mesoamerica, especially in the Central Valley of Mexico as well as the Toltec regions from Tula to Chichén Itzá. Ball courts of the type found across the Maya, Toltec, Aztec, Zapotec, Mixtec, and Totonac regions also made their way to El Salvador, as did the *talud-tablero* pyramid construction technique most well known in the Totonac site at El Tajín, Veracruz.

The spread of northern Mesoamerican influence to El Salvador took place largely through travel along the Pacific Coast, where climate and topography most suited overland movement over long distances, as opposed to the Caribbean side. There were many causes for this expansion southward, most likely spurred on by the need for resources as Mexican populations grew, as well as the demand for cacao, which was abundant in El Salvador. These interests may have led to military expeditions to the south, culminating in the Pipils displacing the Maya as the dominant force in western El Salvador.

Salvadoran trade was vibrant both within the Pipil empire and beyond. The Post-Classic trade era was interregional, with networks extending as high north as the Aztec capital of Tenochtitlan (site of current-day Mexico City). As it existed under the Aztec system, the Pipils had a hierarchical market mindset that provided the elite with privileged access to goods and services, money (cacao), as well as allowed them to control distribution, collect tribute, control the obsidian trade (that came mostly from Guatemala and Mexico), and officiate at markets.

The markets were bustling displays in those days as Indian markets tend to be today and they traded then much of what they trade now. Pipil society produced varieties of pottery, textiles, metals, art, honey, wax, cotton, beans, squash, corn, cacao, tobacco, chilies, tomatoes, peanuts, manioc, avocadoes, potatoes, and other regional items. The Pipils most likely introduced *tortillas* (cornmeal patties) and the *comal* (griddle used for cooking tortillas) to El Salvador, albeit in their unique Salvadoran way. For example, unlike the Mexican tortilla, which is thin and light, the Salvadoran tortilla was narrower, heavier, and thicker, and was most likely the precursor to the Salvadoran national dish, the *pupusa*. The *tamal* was already in El Salvador when the Pipils first arrived and continues to be consumed by Salvadorans today. Beverages such as *pulque* (an alcoholic drink from the maguey cactus), *pozole* (hominy soup), and *atole* (a nonalcoholic drink made from corn) were common back then as they are now.

Of all foods, maize took precedence and was produced all over El Salvador. Maize was used for commerce during pre-Columbian times and for commerce and tribute during Spanish colonialism. Cojutepeque, Cuscatlán (San Salvador post-1529), Ateos, Nahuizalco, Ilopango, Nonualco, Santa Ana, Texacuango, Chalchuapa, and many others were important centers of maize production. However, bean and chili production was mostly limited to central and western Cuscatlán province both during pre-Columbian and colonial times. This fact made Cuscatlán important for tribute to Spanish Crown authorities and landed elites as it produced half of the bean tribute and over 90 percent of the chili tribute for all El Salvador in the mid-sixteenth century.

Salt making and dried fish also played important roles in the Pipil market. The Pacific Coast inhabitants of most of Central America used a technique based on the use of canoes that collected salty marshland soils, followed by boiling the substance down over fire pits. This practice was not only the most ancient salt producing method but it continued throughout the colonial era when salt was used for tribute for the benefit of Spanish merchants and the Crown. The settlements producing salt also depended on the production of dried fish and these sites were located both on the coast and inland.

Cacao was also highly prized in El Salvador as it was used for currency as well as a drink. The drink was usually mixed with chilies rather than honey and people added the food coloring of *achiote* to make the drink resemble blood. This drink was the exclusive terrain of the elite as with much else in Pipil society and its importance for ceremonies paralleled the significance of the cacao bean to the much mightier Aztecs of Mexico. After the conquest, cacao was so coveted that all 14 departments of the western province of Izalcos produced it for tribute and cacao production soon made its way to central El Salvador where it had been absent under the Pipil and Lenca reigns.

Honey and wax represented two more elements to Salvadoran trade prior to the arrival of the Spanish. Although not a mainstay of the tribute system, these products still created demand among consumers, and the Spanish officials with land holdings and Indian workers in the departments of Cojutepeque, Zacatecoluca, and Nahuizalco, profited from them.

The most important indigenous crop for Spanish colonial commerce, indigo, had been produced and traded in El Salvador prior to the arrival of the conquistadors, especially in the central part of the country. Initially, indigo did not attract the Spanish merchants as much as cacao, but by the 1560s indigo production increased in tandem with cotton production as the textile industry expanded. The most important zone for textile production was the Paraíso Basin where cotton and indigo converged as the Spanish forced nearly every Pipil settlement to produce both crops. The Spanish would benefit from many other indigenous products, but indigo was number one overall throughout the colonial era.

The Pipils also specialized in many different crafts, highly sought after by locals and Spanish alike. Stone ornaments, tools, weapons, pottery, finished bone products for ornamentation and tools, gourd and wooden artifacts, woven mats, feather work (for Quetzal feather headdresses), and various other woven materials consumed millions of hours of work every year within Pipil households and markets. The weaving was left to the women and the stone work to the men. Chipped stone was mostly done with obsidian from the north and places such as Santa Maria and Cihuatán were well known for having obsidian workshops that made high quality implements such as blades and other crafts.

Located in the Paraíso Basin near the Lempa River, these sites also most likely produced significant quantities of pottery. As with other crafts, tasks were divided by gender, and often are to this day. For example, women are the principal potters today. Interestingly enough, despite millennia of experience, Salvadoran pottery, as with many other Mesoamerican products, did not benefit from the potter's wheel. In fact, they had no use for the wheel outside of children's toys, and this disadvantage would serve the Spanish well during the conquest. The site at Apopa specialized in ceramics and Nahuizalco even paid ceramics as tribute to the Spanish due to their high level of specialization for many years prior to the conquest. The Pipils also specialized in making *petates* (straw mats for sleeping), which were sold at markets before the Spanish arrived and used for both markets and tribute in the northwestern regions of El Salvador during colonial times. Today, the important pre-Columbian Pipil sites at Nahuizalco and Cojutepeque continue to produce large amounts of *petates* and other straw products for tourists and locals alike.

Wood weapons were also abundant and their designers were either specialists in military hardware or the warriors themselves. They produced spear shafts, *atlatls* (implement with assisted mechanism for launching a spear), *macanas* (obsidian bladed weapons), and other implements, none of which could compete well with Spanish weaponry, which depended on steel, firearms, and horses. The Pipil elite also depended on tribute in the form of military service, food, cotton, cacao, gold, and obsidian, and the Spanish plugged into this already functioning system and expanded it upon arrival.

As with the Spanish, religion was of the utmost importance to the Pipils. According to the Spanish official Garcia del Palacio in a letter written to King Philip II in 1576, Pipil society was based on religious structures that may have concentrated power into the hands of a single entity that promoted the use of ritual human sacrifice not uncommon throughout Mesoamerica. Like their Mexican brethren far to the north, Pipil families were organized into *calpullis*, an equivalent to a clan, with chiefs who served as leaders, representatives, and advisors. Each community held their chiefs and priests in high honor. The hierarchy was led by a *tecti* or "lord" (possibly borrowed from the Aztec term for the same, *teuctli*), who presided over important ceremonies and rituals and provided guidance to the citizenry and was given charge of all sacred books. The two prominent Pipil deities have parallels in Mexican traditions as well: Quetzalcoatl (the feathered serpent) and Itzcueye (the earth mother goddess of Gulf Coast origin). By the middle of the sixteenth century the social, economic, cultural, and political landscape of El Salvador had completely changed as the region lost its original structures and boundaries and found new ones erected in their place due to the arrival of the Spanish.

THE CONQUEST

The Pipil and Lenca soon came under attack from forces with which they could not contend. In 1492, Columbus made landfall at several Caribbean islands, including Hispaniola and Cuba, the latter being 100 miles from Mexico. Central American shores were not far off and in 1502 Columbus arrived in the Gulf of Honduras on the Caribbean side of the isthmus, making Central America the first location where Europeans encountered evidence of advanced civilization in the Americas. This was still two decades prior to the Conquest of Mexico, the first of such major conquests over indigenous empires to occur in the Americas. In 1508, Spanish ships discovered the Yucatan Peninsula and three years later Spanish explorers suffered a devastating attack that left only two survivors in the Yucatec Maya territory. One of them, Jerónimo de Aguilar, would factor into the Conquest of Mexico eight years later when he was rescued by Hernán Cortez and his men. Aguilar, Cortez, and hundreds more Spaniards along with thousands of Indians conquered the Aztec empire in central Mexico in 1521. The following year, Spanish sailors discovered El Salvador.

The first Spaniards to arrive at El Salvador had sailed up from Panama along the Pacific coast on their way to the Spice Islands. They landed temporarily in the Bay of Fonseca, named after a bishop and the president of the Council of the Indies in Madrid, but they did not conquer the Indians. As it was during the pre-Columbian era, El Salvador found itself in a new frontier zone, this time between two competing factions of conquistadors in the 1520s. It rested on both the northern frontier of the region under exploration by conquistadors led by Pedrarias Davila in Panama and the southern frontier of the region coveted by conquistadors in Mexico under Hernán Cortez and Pedro de Alvarado. This type of fierce competition among conquistadors was entirely common in the age of conquest over rich and powerful indigenous kingdoms possessing millions of square miles of territory and subjects, and especially the abundance of gold and silver of the Aztecs and Incas.

In 1524, Cortez's right hand man, Pedro de Alvarado, had conquered Guatemala and set his sights on El Salvador. As had been the case prior to his arrival in Guatemala, Alvarado had an unseen ally that preceded his conquests in El Salvador. The diseases that had spread south from Mexico due to Spanish contact with the Indians had plagued the area from 1519–1524 and as with the Aztecs to the north, the Maya, Pipil, and Lenca to the south had no natural immunities to European diseases. As a result, up to 50 percent of the population died prior to the arrival of the conquistadors in 1524. Other epidemic cycles hit Mesoamerica as a whole in 1545–1548 and 1576–1581, which eliminated the possibility of future effective Indian resistance by reducing the population to approximately 10 percent of its preconquest numbers. Diseases were almost unheard of in the Americas with the possible exception of syphilis prior to the European invasion. Old World diseases of smallpox, measles, typhus, malaria, and yellow fever were the most destructive. The tremendous losses sustained by Native Americans led to the push for African slavery, which further devastated tens of millions of Africans all over the hemisphere in the next four centuries.

Compared to the Conquest of Mexico, in which Cortez cut off the head of the Aztec empire by conquering Tenochtitlán, Alvarado and his fellow conquistadors had to conquer several small kingdoms in Central America such as the Quiches, Kaqchikels, Tzutuhils, Pipils, and Lencas, as well as villages relatively isolated politically from one another. This was the case due to the lack of any cohesive unit of territory governed by one figure head or governing body, so each zone had to be subdued individually. The same was true for Spanish conquistadors coming north from Panama expecting to conquer great kingdoms like that of Mexico. This had the effect of creating areas temporarily outside of Spanish control along the frontier zone in El Salvador and Nicaragua, and this made quashing later Indian revolts somewhat more difficult.

Pedro de Alvarado's name is not welcome in indigenous Central America. Even more so than the reputation of the main conquistadors of Mexico (Hernán Cortez) and Peru (Francisco Pizarro), for the Indians, Alvarado's name is synonymous with terror and brutality due to his relentless wars against the native population. His attacks on the Quiches and Kaqchikels killed thousands and were followed by the branding and enslavement of thousands more. Alvarado entered El Salvador from the west in 1524, and battles between Spaniards, Pipils, and Lencas continued for 15 years. With 250 Spanish troops, 100 horses, and 5,000 Guatemalan allies, Alvarado defeated Salvadoran warriors engaged in traditional as well as guerrilla warfare, securing resounding victories in such places as Sonsonate and Acajutla before moving on to Cuscatlán and Izalcos, two of the most significant Pipil strongholds. However, after failing to secure these last two cities, Alvarado regrouped in Guatemala with the intention of returning during the dry season.

In 1525, Gustavo de Alvarado succeeded in founding the first Spanish settlement at San Salvador and in the following year, the country was secure enough for Pedro to travel all the way through the territory from Guatemala to Honduras. However, upon his return, he had to fight his way through the country against Salvadorans incited to revolt by anti-Alvarado Kaqchikel Maya warriors, many of whom had been part of the original conquest. Finally, on the third conquest attempt, Diego de Alvarado led troops to success in 1528 despite several isolated Indian revolts.

From that point on, El Salvador was safely in Spanish hands. The Spanish slowly gained control over the territory by individually acquiring Indian towns and thus Indian subservience through battle and disease. In 1530, Alvarado's men captured the Lenca territory in the east after fighting with Pedrarias's forces over the territory. The peace did not last long, however. In 1537, a rebellion incited by a chief in Higueres, Honduras shook the Spanish to their core after Indians overran the province of Chaparrastique, leaving the garrison at San Miguel as the only safe haven for Spanish inhabitants. The Spanish took 12 years to put down the revolt in 1547, and the next Indian revolt took place nearly 300 years later, in 1832.

3

The Colonial Period, 1524–1821

THE AFTERMATH OF CONQUEST

With the long age of conquest, El Salvador found itself quickly and forever altered from the very heart of its preconquest foundations. Foreign invaders controlled the territory by force; diseases reduced the Indians to a shadow of their former selves; *adelantados* (first arrivals) governed over Spanish and Indian alike; Indians were forced to work for *encomenderos* (Spanish landlords charged with converting the Indians); the new mixed race *mestizo* (or *ladino*, term used for people of mixed European and Indian blood) increased in numbers; Salvadorans were part of a global market; the corrupt *repartimiento* (no real English translation but referred to system of Indian servitude for the Spanish) system controlled the means of production, African slaves worked for Spanish masters; nonnative animals devastated the landscape; new foods and beverages such as wheat, sugar, olives, coffee, rice, and wine were introduced, and the Catholic Church hierarchy replaced the native religious orders.

Surely, these events occurred in the rest of Latin America as well; but it could be argued that colonialism had a more intense and longer lasting impact on El Salvador than on most of the hemisphere. The colonial period of El Salvador's history technically lasted from 1524 to 1821, when the nation declared its independence from Spain along with the rest of Central America. Colonialism has continued in many ways. Reasons for this abound. For example, the Indian population that had spent the past several thousand years building their own societies experienced the destruction of their culture at the hands of people who cared little about learning about them. Spanish religious practices, forced relocations, forced labor, and church activism led to the loss of Indian identity, breaking down their resistance to oppression and exploitation, even as they lost in battle and in health. In addition, as a small country, there was much less room for economic diversification and thus the territory's development rested on semifeudal foundations that depended almost entirely on the cultivation and sale of indigo for over 300 years. After indigo, El Salvador depended almost entirely on coffee well into the twentieth century. This *monoculture* economy simultaneously plugged El Salvador into the world economy and tied the power structure of the country (the church, the merchants, the government, the landed elite) to the majority poor population in an uneven power relationship. This situation has been difficult to alter down the years and has been symbolized by such elements as the so-called fourteen families and conflicts like *La Matanza* of 1932 and the civil war from 1980–1992. The colonial foundations established a near concrete societal structure that made change for the majority poor all but impossible and therefore armed conflict and oppression became close to inevitable. The story of their colonial foundations follows.

EARLY COLONIAL GOVERNANCE

Once the Spanish had established control over El Salvador, conquistadors were tasked with governing their respective areas of conquest. Known as *adelantados*, the former conquistadors were the first to serve as a colonial administration and thus set the pace for the future municipal governors. The first couple decades of Spanish rule experienced a general lack of organization and El Salvador's location on the margin of Central America limited its inclusion in colonial affairs. The first seat of jurisdiction over Central America was in Comayagua, Honduras, and it was called the Audiencia de Los Confines and had four administrators overseeing the region. By 1542, all of Central America fell under the governance of the Kingdom of Guatemala. By then, there were fully 15 municipalities under the watchful eyes of Crown-appointed colonial officials that ruled as extensions of the Holy Roman Emperor, Charles I (1516–1556).

The Indians were soon subdued under several programs. The Church sent missionaries along with the conquistadors that took over the villages and began to convert the Indians, which made them easier to assimilate under Spanish control. Next, the Spanish set the *encomienda* system in motion. This was a form of virtual enslavement of the Indians that the adelantados who conquered each region controlled. Entire towns and the Indians within them were under the control of individual or multiple Spaniards who had the right to their tribute and were responsible for their conversion and protection. This provided Spaniards with the material with which to trade and pay their royal taxes. The encomienda was an example of how the Spanish were lifted up by the sweat of Salvadoran Indians, who were only pushed further into the ground, and it represents the first stage in the established privilege of the Spanish-rooted minority over the Indian and ladino majority that has become the foundation of Salvadoran inequality to this day. This was not the same system experienced by African slaves, who nonetheless made up a very small proportion of the forced labor in El Salvador. One positive aspect of this was, just like Costa Rica, not much gold or silver was ever found in El Salvador and therefore the Spanish there tended to be agriculturalists instead of miners. At the same time, the Conquest of Peru (1532) provided a tremendous opportunity for conquistadors seeking riches and as a result many Spaniards abandoned the project of El Salvador and went south.

In the process of conquest and colonization, the ladino birth rate outpaced the birth rate of the Indians who were dying faster than they could reproduce, eventually displacing the Indian majority as their numbers fell due to disease, overwork, and battle. And as the races mixed, cultures mixed to create hybrids out of conflict. With food, Europeans and Indians complemented one another's culture such as with Old World limes, oranges, peaches, pineapples, melons, lemons, olives, wheat, rice, and livestock that arrived in El Salvador. The Salvadoran native diet of maize, beans, and squash also became the diet of the Spanish, and native crops of tobacco, cacao, indigo, cotton, honey, wax, achiote, and chilies were also highly coveted by Europeans. However, the Spanish view of these native items was almost purely in terms of seeking to exploit their value either for financial gain or personal desire, and this greed on their part only accelerated the marginalization of the Indians.

As the Spanish acquired more and more territory, their use of large-scale farms altered the traditional use of the soil. Old and New World crops exploited by non-native landowners now occupied large swaths of land previously used by Indians for subsistence and their own trade networks. At the same time, Old World animals would graze and roam across Indian subsistence agricultural land unused to such large beasts as horses, cattle, sheep, goats, and pigs that consumed grasslands and eroded the soil on which the Indians depended for survival. This further exacerbated the already dreadful situation so many withstood after the conquest. Eventually, after tremendous losses of acreage in Indian fertile soil, the Audiencia of Guatemala decreed in 1637 that Indians were allowed to kill any cattle that wondered into their milpas.

The main cities of San Salvador, Santa Ana, and San Miguel were the center of colonial life. Village settlement began with the founding of San Salvador in 1525, and the city subsequently moved to different locations in 1528, 1530, 1538, and 1539, and was later devastated by earthquakes several times. San Miguel was founded in 1530 as the center of the department of Chaparrastique and was almost totally abandoned several times over the course of the sixteenth century due to fire, and attractive opportunities outside of El Salvador such as exploration, conquest, and silver discoveries. El Salvador was mostly a series of small towns serving mostly as way stations and frontier zones with little opportunities for most with the exception of cacao, cotton, and indigo, whose markets were often unreliable and the profits of which went to a concentrated minority. Eventually, San Salvador itself and the surrounding countryside became the most profitable center for the Spanish in all of Central America, even though the region's importance paled in comparison to Mexico and Peru.

An important aspect of Salvadoran settlement was that Spanish and Indian villages were rarely that separate from the very beginning. Spaniards set up homes within existing Indian towns and this pattern was different from the heavy use of *reducciones* in most of Latin America in which several Indian settlements were concentrated into one for the purpose of control. As a result of this different approach in El Salvador, mixture occurred in full force early on and this also accelerated the disruption of Indian life as disease, cattle, and displacement caused their numbers to dwindle. In one study, of 70 eastern Indian villages with a combined population of about 30,000 in 1550, only 52 villages with 8,300 people remained 40 years later, without saying anything of the initial conquest devastation from 1524–1530. Epidemics would continue throughout the century and occasionally plagued populations in those that followed. The importation of African slaves did not overcome these losses as it did in the Caribbean.

HAPSBURG RULE

The first two decades of Spanish settlement and governance were largely experimental in El Salvador. The New Laws of 1542 enacted provisions technically forbidding the unjust exploitation of Indians such as slavery, and the encomienda was severely restricted. These laws responded to voices of Indian defenders such as Father Bartolomé de las Casas who wrote of the conquistadors' actions, but their enforcement was minimal in Central America. While the encomienda faded rapidly as an institution, the *repartimiento* (forced labor draft system) and the *hacienda* (great estate) served to equally exploit the Indian.

Indians also received a separate legal identity within separate institutions from the Spanish. Indian governance even in cases where Spanish and Indians lived in the same area, were governed within a *comunidad* (community) with their own *administrador* (administrator) and several *socios* (assistants) whom the local Indians elected. However, the Indians had very little rights compared to the Spanish who were given de facto legitimacy due to their birthplace or family history. In a case in point, when a volcanic eruption threatened the town of Nejapa in 1658, Indian villagers petitioned Spanish authorities to settle on land near a Spanish hacienda and were rejected on the official reasoning that the *hacendado*'s cattle would harm the Indians' crops. Another problem was even more pressing: in the minds of the Spanish, the indigo mills on those lands were too valuable to be jeopardized by the survival needs of the Indians. Spaniards of the time portrayed the plight of the Indians as a result of their inherent inferiority, and not attributable to Spanish actions. Instead, the Indians' backwardness was viewed as the result of God's will.

This view of the Indians as naturally inferior was supported by many in the church. Monastic orders entered El Salvador in 1551, bringing droves of priests to the region that converted the Indians, oversaw the building of churches (by Indian laborers) and tended to the spiritual needs of their Spanish and Indian parishioners. By the 1570s both San Salvador and Los Izalcos had Dominican and Franciscan monasteries, while only the Franciscans built one in San Miguel on the east end, which was seen as less important than the other two at the time. Unlike the wealthy established church elite in Mexico and Peru, the Church of El Salvador did not excel to such grandiose heights for they mostly subsisted on the gifts and tithes of their modest flocks that were poor Indians and ladinos including a small minority upper class group of Spaniards.

The government making all these changes was the Hapsburg Dynasty that ruled Spain from 1500 to 1700. The Hapsburgs attempted to pull in the reigns on the conquistadors and adelantados of the initial years after the conquest in order to profit more from their colonies and to spread Catholicism. They despised the abusive conquistadors that viewed Latin America as a vast spoil of war to be acquired and exploited at the expense of order, respect for the Crown's authority, and the Indians. This chaotic period soon came to a close with the arrival of Alonso Lopez de Cerrato (1548–1554), who was appointed president of the Audiencia of Guatemala by the Hapsburg Crown to oversee the implementation of the New Laws and to consolidate Crown authority in Central America.

The Laws failed in many ways in Peru and Mexico, as they met with a severe backlash from those profiting from the exploitation of the encomienda and enslavement of Indians. Cerrato stood out because he freed many Indians from slavery and their encomiendas in El Salvador. However, he then awarded privileged access to land and Indian labor to his friends. The repartimiento in particular was able to flourish under his watch, setting in motion the extremely exploitative practice of this institution for the rest of the colonial era.

The Cerrato reforms also represent the beginning of orderly colonial administration in Central America where there was none before despite the high level
of corruption that was able to continue by linking government administration
of labor to the profits of the repartimiento.

Despite the increase in order, the decline of the Indian population did not
slow down until the end of the century. The pandemics of the sixteenth century all accelerated the labor problems and the decline of Indian traditions.
The seventeenth century witnessed a relative stabilization of the Indian population, which eventually began to develop immunities to European diseases
and by the nineteenth century they had mostly recovered their preconquest
numbers. However, El Salvador, unlike Guatemala, Mexico, Peru, Bolivia, Ecuador, and Paraguay, among others, did not experience the continuation of
this upward trend due to the massive repression against indigenous peoples
up through the twentieth century. Guatemala, Ecuador, and Bolivia all have
Indian majorities. Mexico, Honduras, Nicaragua, Peru, Paraguay and others
have between 10 and 50 percent Indian populations. El Salvador has the lowest percentage of native peoples in Central America with only one percent.

The Hapsburgs governed with the intentions of maintaining order in the
colonies and preserving loyalty to the Crown. The colonial authorities under
the Hapsburgs were not expected to govern under the micromanagement of
the Crown but instead to preserve these two qualities. It was a decentralized
governing structure that proved unable to coordinate responses between the
colonies and the metropolis and therefore depended on municipal authorities
for most governmental decision making. The Hapsburg process for leadership
selection followed that the Crown's choice of rulers would loyally carry out
their policies, and therefore positions were not awarded based on ability but
on connections. Through this system, if loyalty was rewarded, then corruption
was allowed as long as it did not interfere with the most important tenet of the
relationship. At the same time, the dynasty's control over the colonies lasted
two centuries. This occurred as long as the mines pumped out enough bullion
to sustain the monarchy and order was preserved. However, weaknesses were
eventually revealed, as the Crown had been engaged in near constant warfare
in Europe and had squandered much of their riches as a result, effectively bol-
stering northern European banks as Spanish power crumbled beneath them.
The Hapsburg loss in the War of Spanish Succession (1701–1712) sealed their
fate and ended this chaotic period of rule, ushering in the age of the Bourbon
dynasty.

LABOR AND EXCHANGE

The economy of Central America did not stand out in comparison to the
rest of Latin America. By and large Central Americans dedicated themselves

to subsistence agriculture in addition to the production of some market commodities for export and internal trade such as indigo, cacao, cotton, and cochineal, all of which had eager consumers but nothing on a par with the demand for products coming from Peru and Mexico.

As an improvement upon the encomienda, colonial authorities used the repartimiento as an incentive to keep colonists in Central America during the tumultuous sixteenth century. Pay for repartimiento laborers was small but they were theoretically to be protected by the Crown. This practice lasted throughout the entire colonial period and in some ways, such as the vagrancy laws, the institution's remnants lasted until the 1930s. Some important differences existed between the encomienda and the new system. Under the encomienda, each *encomendero* had an interest in maintaining their Indians' health, but under the repartimiento there was no relationship of protection between overseer and Indian. Exploitation increased tremendously within the repartimiento system because laborers could be sent to different overseers depending on financial interests, in addition to public works projects. This opened the door to endless schemes involving colonial officials with financial interests who could then utilize the repartimiento labor obligation system for their own advantage, and it was not until the Bourbon Reforms of the eighteenth century that the Crown cracked down on this corrupt practice.

The cotton industry expanded under Spanish rule and the repartimiento system provided an avenue for officials to force Indians to work for their monopoly over the cotton industry. Cotton was harvested in the lowlands of the Kingdom of Guatemala, which included parts of El Salvador, and was then sent up to highlands for weaving. Some cotton went to Mexico, while most was sold in Honduras and El Salvador, which linked it to the rest of the world because it later traded indigo throughout Central America for goods originating in Europe. This laid the groundwork for the trade networks through which El Salvador accelerated its growth during the coffee boom as well, during the late nineteenth century through the twentieth.

With indigo, there was no real monopoly but the repartimiento played a crucial role in maintaining power in the hands of elite planters tied to the colonial government who provided the former with forced labor. Indeed, the entire system depended on a high level of corruption because the Spanish authorities had a hierarchy of direct control over commercial production and labor. The structure of this control was run by colonial governors with a stake in the indigo, who then controlled the municipal authorities (*alcaldes mayores*) who held authority over colonial officials with authority over Indian communities (*corregidores*) who then forced Indian chiefs (*caciques*) to distribute laborers according to the interests of the hierarchy of colonial elites. Spanish officials involved in this scheme were able to use political power to close down competitors, keep wages low, enforce debt and tax collection, use revenues for projects that would suit their commercial needs (road building and construction of buildings, etc.), and use police forces to protect their interests. It was a semi-fiefdom in a quasi-medieval sense of the word, with the added benefit of global commercial connections.

One can see how difficult life must have been for the Indians living as peasants in colonial El Salvador. This is especially clear when we consider the fact that the same officials charged with enforcing laws to protect Indian rights had little interest in doing so when it infringed upon their profits. According to one report by indigo planters in the mid-1600s: "In view of the exhausted and humble condition of the Indians and the greed of those that make demands on them, there are no wickednesses so great that are not perpetrated and the common result is the vexation, oppression and destruction of the Indians despite the many laws intended . . . for the prevention of these excesses."[1] As a result of these policies, further disintegration of Indian communities occurred as the indigo plantations took over Indian land as well as drew in Indian laborers. This would later prove important for the perpetuation of Spanish and elite family dominance in modern times.

There were also African slaves in El Salvador, albeit in relatively small numbers compared to the Caribbean. Thousands of Africans were originally imported to work in the small number of mines, and in 1625, 2,000 rebellious slaves celebrating Holy Week raised fears among the authorities and the population enough to lead to the execution of several of the leaders. They did not rise up again during that year and the authorities viewed them as more apt to revolt than the Indians, who had been subdued the previous century. By the end of the eighteenth century, only 600 African slaves were left in El Salvador.

This system of Spanish exploitation, developing over the course of three centuries of Spanish rule, could not be reversed easily, and when coffee came along in the mid-nineteenth century, this system of inequality only increased, further marginalizing the population, and leading closer to the type of civil conflict witnessed in the twentieth century. Indians of the repartimiento even had to pay tribute in the form of goods they produced and the money they earned to the local magistrates. In addition, the Spanish took advantage of already existing labor divisions along gendered lines: women produced textiles and thread in the economy whereas the men mostly worked in the fields. They even took advantage of existing labor traditions among Indians who already cultivated cotton, cacao, and indigo, as well as spinning and weaving textiles, and therefore the Spanish effectively took what already existed to a new level by exploiting their labor for their own profit. In return, finished goods flowed back into El Salvador from other parts of the Spanish colonies as well as Europe and Asia.

Thus, the repartimiento was not only corruption, exploitation, and hardship. It also integrated all of Central America together and with the global economy, and these connections have continued to grow ever since. The colonies were also divided according to their regional specialty through this program. Guatemala and Nicaragua produced cotton, Chiapas and Guatemala wove it, El Salvador produced indigo, Honduras produced silver, and silver and indigo went north to Mexico, south to Peru, and east to Europe. One important point about this economic system is the fact that Spanish exploitation of already existing traditions of production actually helped to perpetuate the survival of a small number of indigenous traditions somewhat. For example, the demand for indigenous-produced goods during this period helped make the Indians a viable economic resource well worth preserving and therefore this provided an incentive for the Spanish authorities to protect their own investments. This did not usually translate into protection for the individual Indians, but instead it meant protection of their cultural goods that could bring profit to the Spanish. Tourists benefit from this today, as do indigenous producers, as a traveler can witness the array of Indian goods still produced in El Salvador.

One major Indian product later produced by the Spanish was cacao. The highly prized nature of this crop, mostly grown on the south side of the volcanoes of El Salvador and Guatemala, was also sought after by the Spanish who realized that the Indian farmer, with the experience of many generations, was the best suited for its cultivation. Even by the 1630s, a full century after the conquest, cacao beans were of great value both for the drink *chocolatl* and for its use as currency. The Spaniards almost immediately sought to expand its trade and eventually through adding sugar it became the treat most sought after the world over to this day. In fact, the production grew so much that Sonsonate district—especially Izalco—produced more than any other part of the Americas. Eventually competition from Venezuela and Ecuador displaced El Salvador's dominance, but cacao still played an important role there into the eighteenth century.

As opposed to cacao, which was controlled by the Indians, indigo was controlled by the Spanish. In a desire to compete on the world market with the Dutch, Portuguese, and English, the Spanish sought indigo lands in Latin America and El Salvador was the most important producer in the hemisphere. By the eighteenth century, Central America exported between 500,000 and 1 million pounds of indigo to Europe annually. El Salvador is well suited for indigo production particularly for its low elevation volcanic slopes around Santa Ana, San Salvador, San Vicente, and San Miguel. It was mostly grown on either flat or gradual inclines and after harvest was processed in an *obraje* (mill) where it processed into large 214 pound cubes known as *zurrones*. As cattle did not disturb the plant, the two often occupied the same tracts of land, providing the indigo farmer with an additional source of income. Due to the fact that the indigo *hacendados* also possessed cattle that would roam beyond their property, the Indian, who possessed neither cattle nor indigo for themselves would be forced to accept a reduced swath of land.

Much as was the case with sugar planting cycles in places such as Brazil and Cuba, the Indigo season dictated life across El Salvador during the colonial period. Due to the length of time between planting the *jiquilite* (leaves that produced indigo) in February and March before rains, and the harvests and fairs in September through November, the entire colony worked around the production of indigo. This coincided with the corn cycles as well, thus once indigo planting or harvesting ended, people returned to their milpas to manage planting and harvesting on their communal *ejidos* (common lands) and private farms. However, so dependent on indigo did El Salvador become that by the end of the colonial period the Spanish government had to encourage production of other crops such as cochineal and sugar in order to avoid the problems associated with monoculture economies.

A fundamental aspect of the monoculture economy developing in El Salvador was the *hacienda* or great estate. The hacienda held a large parcel of land (up to several thousand acres) and was owned by the Spanish and Creole elite sectors of society. They tended to have up to several hundred workers as well, many of whom lived on the land owned by the hacendado without ownership of their own land. These would produce large quantities of indigo for processing and export, and later many became towns themselves due to their enormous size. There were 442 haciendas in the Intendancy of San Salvador (the territory of modern-day El Salvador) at the end of the colonial period. Their sizes were enormous and varied wildly, extending up to over 14,000 acres. They averaged 2,000 acres a piece and thus these 442 estates made up one-third of the total acreage of El Salvador. The haciendas were also realms unto themselves, nearly free from regulations. Their sizes outreached that of many modern towns and as such wealthy people lived rather freely in groups of many families at times. There were only two different forms of land use during the colonial period, the other being the *pueblo,* which contained communally held ejidos worked by the peasants.

As the repartimiento lost momentum briefly in the late 1600s, demand for forced labor had to be met by other methods. *Debt peonage* was soon instituted and took off under the Bourbon Reforms of the next century. The *peon* was at the bottom of the socioeconomic ladder simply through the status of his nonelite, peasant parents and this status tended to pass itself on through the generations. A peon was usually an Indian or a ladino from the countryside with no education or refined skills and was therefore subject to exploitation by the elites of El Salvador as was the case with the repartimiento. Those peons indebted to landowners were often forced to remain as such for many years and even throughout a lifetime. The hacendado who controlled a peon's labor often owned the *tienda de raya* (company store), the peon's only source of goods and services, and as such the landowner kept many workers perpetually indebted.

The land tenure system in El Salvador thus instituted a patron-client or master-man arrangement that grew roots in all of Latin America during the colonial period. These developed out the feudal mentality of the landed elite system that was tied to the state that enforced the laws surrounding the encomienda, the repartimiento, and the debt peonage labor obligations keeping the peons continually at the bottom of the socioeconomic ladder. In addition, this system contributed to *caudillismo,* whereby a strong man would emerge as a de facto regional leader due to his status as a wealthy landowner with the power to both help and hurt the prospects of large numbers of people within his realm of influence.

With the potential for profit came the need for protection, and therefore the Crown took measures to defend El Salvador from menacing elements such as English pirates. Piracy in particular menaced the Spanish Caribbean and Spanish mainland in the sixteenth century, and Sir Francis Drake took Jamaica in 1568, making Central America a potential target of his pillaging. In fact, he made his way close to the coast of El Salvador in 1579 and in 1586, which caused colonist militias to prepare their defenses. The first actual attacks came in 1682 at the delta to the Lempa River, causing citizens to flee inland and ladino militias to take up arms to occupy villages as far inland as Chalatenango in the north, many of which remained there into the eighteenth century. The pirates intended to interdict bullion and indigo and by the mid-eighteenth century, with the expansion of indigo production, increased defense and new paths for transportation of indigo were necessary to evade capture and pillage. Until this point, Salvadoran products were taken via the port of Acajutla to the port of Acapulco in Mexico, then unloaded and taken overland to the port of Veracruz where they sailed to Cadiz, Spain. By 1760, indigo traveled overland from El Salvador to Guatemala to the fortified port of Omoa, Honduras before sailing to Havana, Cuba and then on to Cadiz. Troops from El Salvador were often delegated to accompany these shipments to Havana for the protection of the indigo.

Throughout the sixteenth and seventeenth centuries, Hapsburg rule under Kings Charles I, Phillip II (1556–1598), Phillip III (1598–1621), Phillip IV (1621–1665), and Charles II (1665–1700) was disorganized yet relatively stable in terms of internal order and progress for the privileged minority living within El Salvador. Nevertheless, the Crown's relatively relaxed attitude toward government caused a significant decay of Spanish power in the minds of critics. For example, the project that created the above mentioned new route for transporting indigo was the result of proactive central planning on the part of the new dynasty, the Bourbons, and symbolized the eighteenth-century Bourbon era reforms that altered the face of Salvadoran affairs tremendously, to which we turn next.

THE BOURBON ERA

The initial well-known Bourbon Reforms were not fully implemented under Phillip V (1700–1724). It was not until the enlightened rule of Charles III (1759–1788) that the said reforms were instituted on a wide scale and these were characterized by major differences between the former Hapsburgs and the Bourbons. Hapsburg decentralization was supplanted by a rigid structure that increased centralized authority in Crown hands. Problems that occurred during the past two centuries began to catch up with Central America as well. Disease had hit Central Americans hard several times (1683, 1686, 1693, 1703, 1705, 1708–1709) as did locusts that plagued the indigo and food crops, and earthquakes further weakened the foundation of the economy. However, by late century, the Industrial Revolution going on in England impacted El Salvador tremendously as indigo demand increased with textile production in both places. The Bourbons had entered the scene under the most challenging and potentially rewarding of circumstances.

By mid-century, Bourbon reforms were firmly in place. The church, previously identified as too powerful, was subsumed under the Crown's control. Tax collection, previously overlooked due to Crown and colony corruption, improved in a manner that harnessed revenues in order to buttress the infrastructure of the colonies. This organization of administration and resources helped to bolster intra-colony trade within Central America, but this expansion of economic freedoms for some did not extend to those at the bottom, whose labor still fell under state control. The Industrial Revolution spurred growth in Central America and this came at the time of greater efficiency in government and economic management by the Bourbons. As a result, Guatemala became the center for and primary beneficiary of the centralization emphasized under the Bourbon Reforms. El Salvador thus increased its connections to Guatemala as the latter increased its power vis-à-vis the former.

As indigo production increased, so did Guatemala and El Salvador's attraction, which drew in large numbers of immigrants. Many of the future elite family names arrived at this time with men such as Gaspar Juarros, Martín Barrundia, Gregorio Urruela, José Piñol, and Juan Fermín de Aycinena (1729–1796). The most notable of these new immigrants was Aycinena, who arrived in Guatemala in 1754 and soon acquired a large portion of the indigo trade within El Salvador. By 1781, he bought the highest noble title of *marquesado* and his financial connections extended to Europe and throughout Spanish America. The Aycinena family controlled trade in Central America by mid-century, serving as public and private banker, and eventually moved for independence from Spain while favoring Britain as its main partner by the turn of the century. After independence, the Aycinena family was still dominant and continued to have a role in the Guatemalan elite.

The arrival of Aycinena occurred in tandem with the arrival of new *penin-sulars* (Spaniards by birth) to El Salvador that quickly led to hostilities with the *creole* (Spaniards born in the Americas) elites. The creoles had spent centuries developing and maintaining considerable power along with the existing peninsulars prior to the Bourbon Reforms. Now that competition increased, violence erupted, the worst of which occurred in El Salvador in 1755 in vicious attacks against each side. Peninsulars were considered superior to and more loyal than the creoles and were therefore given privileged access to government, land, trade, and labor. As a result, peninsulars became more entrenched in the capital city of Guatemala and used their power to secure more Indians for labor, used more colonial revenues for building roads for transporting their indigo, and kept themselves out of the watchful eye of the law, all of which gave a disadvantage to their creole competitors.

The most far reaching reforms came in 1763 beginning with changes made to the colonial administrative structure by the *visitador* to Mexico, Jose de Galvez (1754–1762) and other visitadores that followed. For example, the tax system was streamlined to eliminate abuses in the tributary system against Indians and to increase Crown revenues, whereas prior to the reforms local officials had extracted tribute for themselves in trade materials rather than silver. However, a major problem with these reforms was that the establishment of the tobacco monopoly by the Crown set up a system whereby tobacco producers in Costa Rica, Honduras, and Guatemala could profit well from the leaf and the Salvadoran rich were increasingly taxed to support this industry even though they were not allowed to profit from it directly.

The repartimiento system ended as result of the continuation of the Bourbon Reforms at the end of the eighteenth century in the hopes of curbing more corruption and excessive profiting. This institution was seen as a violation of the free market ideals of the time because officials themselves could divert forced labor drafts to the projects that benefited their investments the most, thus effectively shutting down their competitors through artificial means. The alcaldes mayores involved in the indigo trade unfairly allocated laborers to large haciendas over small landholders. Of the 500 haciendas, only 78 received all 3,284 Indian laborers in 1807, for example, and this demonstrated the level of privilege enjoyed by those elite peninsulars with government connections. Eventually, the trade was broken down into 15 *partidos* from the original 4 in El Salvador, theoretically improving the protection of labor and efficiency of production through more bureaucratic management that was supported by increased tax collection. They were San Salvador, Olocuilta, Zacatecoluca, San Vicente, Usulután, San Miguel, Gotera, San Alejo, Sensuntepeque, Opico, Tejutla, Chalatenango, Santa Ana, Metapán, and Cojutepeque.

Towns soon came under the management of *ayuntamientos* (municipal councils, also known as *cabildos*). Ayuntamientos also helped control the Montepio de Cosecheros de Añil, a crediting agency for indigo entrepreneurs and these two together facilitated business owners' access to government, which Bourbon Reforms actually encouraged. In order to manage these further divisions of government, the Crown appointed *intendantes* to oversee the new Intendancy of El Salvador that served as its own governmental unit with the Kingdom of Guatemala as a result of these reforms.

El Salvador far surpassed the rest of Central America in indigo production, yielding over three-fourths of the total in 1807. People were able to purchase European finished goods through indigo sales as long as prices continued with demand. Indigo hit a boom stage in the late eighteenth century and this became the central driver of the Central American economy. This consequently brought merchants into competition with the Crown in both the financing of and profiting from the trade. It also forced producers in El Salvador into conflict with Guatemalan merchants who set indigo prices as well as controlled their loans, which were based on annual indigo yield potentials, giving the Guatemalan merchants a significant amount of control over El Salvador. Militia units also increased their control especially with the increased threat of piracy such as when British pirates ransacked 79,000 pounds of indigo from Acajutla in 1799. The increased importance of the militia led to the privilege for military classes known as *fueros,* an additional cause for animosity between the peninsular and creole classes that would come out in the years to come.

In general, the elites of El Salvador benefited from this type of privilege. So elite was this class that there was no university, and literacy was limited to them essentially. Education rarely existed, and elite education took place at the Universidad de San Carlos in Guatemala. In 1768, Archbishop Pedro Cortes y Larraz (1712–1786) visited El Salvador and found no schools. In response, in the 1770s, the Audiencia of Guatemala ordered the building of primary schools, but the lack of education as a cultural value in El Salvador made finding qualified teachers difficult. The culture depended almost entirely on indigo and subsistence agriculture, with a very small elite and professional class. The trades people found work in mostly agriculture, with some musicians, blacksmiths, shoemakers, bakers, tailors, silversmiths, construction workers, dyers, painters, carpenters, hat makers and weavers as well. The professional class was made up of 4 lawyers, 4 physicians, 12 surgeons, and 7 druggists. The city of San Salvador had a population of 15,000 and 614 were Spaniards with a near dominance over the elite class along with many creoles but excluding the darker-skinned majority.

The elites also had more access to urban areas that possessed more opportunities such as education. Urban education was also easier to promote because it had more connections with the outside world that contained the world of international trade. Therefore, those with urban connections inherently had more of a sense of the necessity of schooling as well as experienced less resistance from peasant and middle income rural traditionalists without these connections. Unfortunately, the initial attempts by the state to force education on people utterly failed. In 1800, La Escuela de la Republica became the first legitimate school to open in San Salvador and was a beacon to the rest of El Salvador. By 1803, Archbishop Luis de Peñalver y Cardenas (1749–1810) reported only one real teacher in the entire intendancy encompassing modern-day El Salvador, which was at La Escuela de la República, and there were only 500 pupils in the entire colony. By 1807, the number of students had tripled, but only to four percent of the eligible students, and while three races were allowed to attend, the Spanish and ladino student numbers far surpassed that of the Indians. Of course, the lessons of the day were not worth much to students anyway when considering that the curriculum consisted of memorization, prayers, and handwriting. El Salvador's education standards have improved gradually since then, but still can not compete with most of Latin America.

THE INDIGO DECLINE AND THE ROAD TO INDEPENDENCE

Events beyond and within Central America began to hurt El Salvador's indigo sales by the end of the eighteenth century. A 1798 war between Spain and England halted most trade between England and the colonies, thus severing a vital link in the indigo trade. Indigo growers depended on loans from Guatemalan merchants based on the previous year's sales and with the losses from 1798 the harvest of 1799 dropped considerably as did those of the following years. That first year's losses set in motion a downward spiral in indigo that did not recover for two decades. Locust attacks on indigo plantations in 1802 and 1803 only hurt this further and increased overhead for indigo producers such as taxation levels and cleanliness requirements meant Salvadoran producers could not compete with the prices and quality of indigo coming from Venezuela and India. By 1806–1808, annual production dropped nearly in half and although it recovered somewhat the following year, it dropped again by the 1809–1813 period, and then declined again from 1814–1818 to nearly a third that produced from 1791–1795.

The effects of this decline had quick repercussions that would reverberate for a generation. Many indigo property loans were called in and Salvadoran producers lost their plantations to Guatemalan merchants owning their loans. In fact, it was in this manner that Juan Fermín de Aycinena acquired a large portion of his indigo territory, and he eventually possessed one-sixth of all the indigo lands in the Kingdom of Guatemala.

This decline also brought down Honduran mining interests, as well as Guatemalan cotton and indigo. The indigo boom of the previous generation had caused El Salvador to become the most densely populated province in Central America and this was made worse by the disproportionate acreage of arable land dedicated to indigo rather than food, which was instead imported from other Central American provinces. With the indigo decline, food producers were negatively affected, as were its consumers in El Salvador whose purchasing power fell. As these losses cycled out of control, the Crown also felt the pinch and responded by consolidating its debts between 1804 and 1808, which further exacerbated the already tense atmosphere between peninsulars on the side of the Crown and creoles seeking less Crown authority and more autonomy.

Local autonomy had been developing under creole auspices during the colonial era. The concept of municipal sovereignty has been studied at length by scholars and revolves around the fact that Spanish colonialism did not foster greater regional identities or cohesiveness and instead cultivated smaller regional identities and thus sovereignty resting on *cabildos* (city councils). This explains many of the problems associated with Salvadoran transition to independence as well, as identity and action were largely limited to the town level, albeit loyalty to the Crown did exist. This concept mattered especially in moments of crisis for the imperial administration, such as in 1808 when Napoleon deposed Ferdinand VII and towns worked locally to preserve their foundations.

The first cracks in the foundations had indeed revealed themselves long before the end of the eighteenth century. As Enlightenment thinkers in Europe flourished and their works translated into Spanish, the elite circles of Central America started thinking of progressive politics. The indigo decline did not help Spanish colonial prospects either and nor did the 1808 expulsion of King Ferdinand VII (1813–1833) from the throne of Spain by Napoleon. In fact, El Salvador would be spared most of the bloodshed that engulfed the larger centers of colonial power in Latin America from Mexico to Chile, where independence revolts convulsed the hemisphere from 1810–1825, even though some fighting did take place in El Salvador.

The conflicts in El Salvador had to do with internal politics specific to Central America as well as external politics general to the hemisphere. For example, the president of the Guatemalan Audiencia from 1811–1817, José de Bustamante, became the chief opponent of the aforementioned Marquis de Aycinena, as Bustamante represented the state and Aycinena represented liberal merchant interests fed up with Spanish regulations. This problem expanded into a liberal-conservative clash, as the liberals sought to expand their own freedom of commerce with Europe, especially England, who was a top competitor with Spain. Meanwhile, Napoleon's invasion of 1808 led to the creation of the liberal Cortes de Cadiz and their liberal constitution of 1812 called for further liberalized administration in the colonies. This tied Bustamante's hands because the Cortes ended the colonial tribute from Central America that was used to finance his government, even as the merchant class led by

Aycinena opposed his trade regulations. Bustamante received little help from the Cortes to back up his enforcement of the law in general even as creoles and peninsulars became more divided over the Independence wars erupting in Mexico and South America.

Rebellion soon hit El Salvador in 1811. Inspired by the revolt in Mexico led by the liberal firebrand priest Miguel Hidalgo y Costilla, and fed up with heavy economic losses, leading liberal elite families led by Father José Matías Delgado (1767–1832), took over the armory of San Salvador and deposed the intendante of the province of San Salvador. Bustamante sent militias down from Guatemala led by José Aycinena and José María Peinado who put down the rebellion and installed Peinado as intendante. This example of Guatemala-El Salvador hostility signaled future problems within Central America in the nineteenth century that had their roots in the eighteenth.

By 1814, Ferdinand VII was released from prison and back on his throne and his counterrevolution expelled the Cortes de Cadiz from power in favor of Ferdinand's more conservative policies. This bolstered Bustamante's hand in Central America as he clamped down on contraband and enforced the general rule of law. However, in an effort to mend fences with the merchant classes and perhaps to reward them for putting down the Salvadoran revolt in 1811, Ferdinand VII had Bustamante ousted and the Aycinena liberals were able to recover their prominence that Bustamante had reduced. The Aycinena liberals then led the movement toward Central American independence that culminated with the Acts of Independence in 1821.

However, first the Liberal Revolution of 1820 in Spain reverted policies back to the 1812 Constitution and inspired the liberal leaders Aycinena (Guatemala) and Delgado (El Salvador) to take control of the provincial deputation in charge of delegating regional authority, instituting a structure in which liberal Guatemalans made the laws instead of Spanish loyalists. The president of the Guatemalan Audiencia, Carlos de Urrutia Montoya y Matos (1818–1821) soon faced the same problems as Bustamante when liberals in Spain restricted his actions and liberals in Central America resisted his rule. He refused to carry out liberal directives from Spain and to participate in deputation proceedings, as was his general attitude toward the creole liberal movement. As independence was close to unfolding in Mexico in 1821, Urrutia stepped down and Gabino Gainza (1753–1829), a liberal Spaniard, took control.

An interesting aspect of this last decade is that unlike the rest of Latin America, Central America did not force the Spanish out with a war for independence. Instead, they slowly transitioned away from Spanish authority through a complex process involving independent action in reliance upon municipal sovereignty as well as incorporation of the Cortes liberal laws of 1812. The Cortes decreed an end to Indian tributes, expanded the franchise for nonwhites, and provided popular elections for local government. At the same time, the reliance on municipal rather than national governing structures that became even more difficult to break during the 1810s because of the turmoil going on within the Spanish colonial government and the competition between municipal and national governance made future Central American cohesion all the more difficult. Because the towns had become self-reliant out of necessity and enablement by the Cortes, it was difficult to break down those walls in favor of giving up power to a national government headquartered far away.

The end of the colonial period also witnessed a widespread loss of support for the Crown from the essential conservative and merchant classes who grew concerned that Spain could no longer help the economic depression. Thus, many elites met in Guatemala to discuss independence and decided to let Mexico lead the way, declaring independence for the United Provinces of Central America as a unified nation on September 15, 1821. The new government of the Junta Consultiva Provisional allowed Spanish citizens to leave with their own fortunes, creating a brain drain and loss of revenues, with the treasury already gone. The nation's first president, Gabino Gainza called for Mexican annexation in 1822 in order to preserve the union, essentially hoping that Mexico would take over as benefactor and protector where Spain had left off. Soon, however, divisions between Guatemalans and Salvadorans led to Guatemala's invitation to Mexican emperor Iturbide to send troops to invade El Salvador in 1822. A combined force of Guatemalan and Mexican troops were beat back by the Salvadorans and left the territory, thus initiating the union under the least unifying of conditions.

The era after the defeat of the Mexican-Guatemalan invasion bolstered the spirits of Salvadorans who now had a reason for confidence in the face of adversity. They quickly had more reason for optimism, as the 1823–1826 indigo cycle recovered and exceeded the peak years of the colonial era booms. In 1826, El Salvador sold 1.2 million pounds of indigo due to freer trade and the end of war (briefly), which increased demand and prices just as import and export prices went down. Growth on this scale would ebb and flow throughout the century, as did armed and peaceful conflicts with El Salvador's neighbors. Overall, Independence meant autonomy from Spanish rule while keeping El Salvador locked in a struggle for power against Guatemala.

NOTE

1. Quoted in David Browning, *El Salvador: Landscape and Society* (Oxford: Clarendon Press, 1972) originally by Garcia Perez, *Memorias para la historia . . .* (1943), vol. I, 241.

4

The Struggle for the Nation, 1821–1871

Independence was not the same for El Salvador as it was for the larger nations of Latin America. As a small yet densely populated province of Central America, its beginnings did not turn out well at all, as not only was the region fragmented into intendancies and provinces prior to independence that shaped the postindependence era, but there were internal class and ideological divisions too deep to resolve immediately. Plus, the newly independent monarchy of Mexico as of early 1822 already had its sights on incorporating Central America into its kingdom and there were many in Central America who agreed as well as disagreed. In 1822, a vote among mostly Guatemalan elites led to the Central American union with Mexico. Salvadoran indigo elites joined up with Guatemalan elites to solidify this direction in government with Guatemala as the regional capital while other Salvadorans resisted, leading to conflict between El Salvador and Guatemala.

This conflict eventually spilled over into a large scale Guatemalan invasion of El Salvador in June 1822. Although Guatemala held the support of Mexico, the Salvadoran troops fought with ferocity in successfully beating back the Guatemalan invaders. However, the Mexican Emperor Agustin de Iturbide would not let this insubordination stand and ordered Mexican commander Vicente Filisofa to attack El Salvador. By January of 1823, Filisofa took San

Salvador, and set up an occupation force in the city and soon El Salvador was officially subsumed under Guatemala under the Mexico-controlled provincial name of Sacatepéquez. However, the Mexican troop presence could not contain the increasingly turbulent atmosphere spreading across Central America as insurgencies flared and Iturbide's rule at home floundered.

The growing conflict only further eroded the already weak financial sectors of El Salvador by cutting off interactions between Guatemala and El Salvador. This hit the indigo sectors especially hard, as many administrators and financiers of the trade were Guatemalan and the plantations were in El Salvador. Therefore, when Salvadorans failed to receive their financing from Guatemala, they went under. In addition, Guatemalans began producing considerable amounts of cochineal, which competed with indigo as a dye. Because Guatemalans produced this alternative dye exclusively, ties were further weakened with El Salvador. Eventually, this parting of ways in some respects opened the door for better commercial ties with Europe. By the 1830s, British merchants were trading directly with El Salvador at indigo fairs in San Miguel and San Vicente, cutting out the middle men in Guatemala as the main merchants and creditors, as British banking interests and investors entered the Salvadoran economy in force.

Once Iturbide was ousted in Mexico in March 1823, the Mexican presence quickly evaporated and by August their troops were out of Central America, which indicated a possible return to normalcy. That same year, Central American independence was declared by the Asamblea Nacional Constituyente. The following year the Provincias Unidas de Centro America was created and its first president, Manuel Jose Arce, a beloved Salvadoran with a history of independence-oriented resistance beginning in 1811, was elected under a liberal constitution in 1825 with the support of the Mexican commander Filisofa, whose influence had continued in the region as a means of supporting the liberal cause to balance against the elite Aycinenas of Guatemala. President Arce had previously been involved in a resistance movement in 1811, which was then followed by other Central American provinces. He asserted that because Ferdinand had abdicated his power, then the Spanish colonial authorities presiding over the government in Central America lacked legitimacy and therefore the power of government rested in the municipal *cabildos*.

The unified nation was soon officially named La Republica Federal de Centroamerica and included Costa Rica, Nicaragua, Honduras, El Salvador, and Guatemala. However, there was little unification in practice, as each nation held a special hostility for at least one other nation, and this animosity lasted well into the twentieth century and continues in some ways to this day. Costa Ricans and Nicaraguans, Salvadorans and Guatemalans, Hondurans and Salvadorans, all have historical problems with one another that have led to countless wars that have brought little more than prolonged periods of grief for all involved. The considerable lack of infrastructure in the early years of the fledgling nation also allowed smuggling to increase as revenues fell sharply and spending climbed with the new bureaucracy of government that placed Guatemala at the center of power with the most control over federal resources.

Civil war soon broke out between competing factions within Central America. The centuries-old rivalry between El Salvador and Guatemala in particular led to a particularly gruesome toll on El Salvador. While Guatemala suffered 2,291 deaths, El Salvador lost 2,546 people in the civil war from 1826–1842, while Nicaragua, Costa Rica, and Honduras lost 1,203, 144, and 682, respectively. The immense population density of El Salvador made for a much harsher situation there during the war, with literally every aspect of life affected adversely across the country. This was similar to the situation Salvadorans suffered during the civil war of 1980–1992, when the country's population was much higher. El Salvador would begin its independence era with its economy and society shaped by the devastation of war.

An illustrative example of this devastation was the 1828 Guatemalan occupation and destruction of eight Salvadoran towns, which led to the loss of 1,286 buildings due to the actions of Guatemalan troops. This occupation forced Salvadoran officials to enact laws of obligatory conscription of soldiers in order to defend the country from further attacks. However, this action only caused further declines in the economy and put undue strains on families. Indeed, fully three percent of the Salvadoran labor force was killed during the war. Civil wars also caused droves of people to flee to the countryside to find whatever new land they could in order to subsist, and this problem led to Indian revolts in Ahuachapan in 1842 and 1854, and by the relatively united Nonualco tribe, led by Anastasio Aquino, which lost a fight for independence in the vicinity of San Vicente and Zacatecoluca over the course of a three month struggle from 1832–1833. This battle may have represented a simple blip on the screen of Salvadoran history, but its symbolic significance can not be understated. The constant struggle of the indigenous population due to their oppression by the lighter skinned classes of ladinos and whites found its way toward armed struggle that year.

It is essential to recognize that the struggle had deep colonial roots. The initial fighting had broken out in 1814 due to Indian resistance to tribute collection by authorities who had grown accustomed to this privilege for three centuries. And even though the resistance was quickly subdued by those defending the traditional authorities, one interesting twist on this event is that it is believed that the Indians learned of the illegality of the tribute from a priest. As we shall see much later, it was the clergy who made up a large portion of the ideological resistance to the military authorities in the 1960s, 1970s, and 1980s, a position that led to many of their deaths.

Returning to the Indian uprising, the Anastasio Aquino revolt of 1833 signified one of the great contradictions of independence in Latin America in general. Independence from Spain did not equal Indian independence simply by virtue of the action itself. Oppression against Indians now possessed another element: the lack of church protection. Whereas one of the only avenues of protection for the Indians used to be the Crown, and with the Spanish Crown gone, the Indian population became subject to further losses in land and life by the new independence leadership and those that followed. The nationalist leadership sought to exploit as much land as possible and therefore moved to privatize large tracts of land that had been under the protection of the Crown for the purposes of continued indigenous usage.

Labor conditions also became worse under the new leaders, and this more than likely provoked the Aquino uprising. Anastasio Aquino and his brother Blas were indigo workers on a hacienda when Blas was punished via the stocks. It was well understood that forced labor of Indians was commonly practiced and this occurred not only on the indigo haciendas but in the regular Salvadoran army as well. When Indian troops were used to put down a ladino uprising against the government in October of 1832, and ladino-Indian clashes erupted in San Miguel in January 1833 with massive suppression of the Indians by the government, Aquino and his followers decided to rise up from Santiago Nonualco. Aquino's guerrillas were particularly offended by forced conscription of Indians fighting for the elite's cause and their initial attacks concentrated on liberating the Indian conscripts and their weapons in order to build a base for a continued battle against the state.

The first major battles against government forces were successful and signaled the possibility that Aquino's men might take the capital if they so chose. However, they decided to conquer lesser towns such as San Vicente and Zacatecoluca, thus giving the military a window of time and space to recover. Although Aquino took San Vicente twice in February, his movement was quickly put down at the end of that month, and he was executed in July.

War also led to more protectionist economic policies against non-Salvadoran businesses, which can be seen as both a possible benefit and a possible mistake. The action was partly in response to the loss of labor from the war, which played a role in the drop in the price of indigo by 50 percent from 1828–1832. This happened even as exports suffered devastating losses by dipping from 1.2 million pounds in 1826 to just 873,750 pounds in 1834 and it continued to fall into the 1840s. For example, in 1828, London paid 10s.4d. per pound for indigo, and in the 1840s it fetched a price of 4s.3d. Unfortunately, Salvadoran indigo would not recover its prewar production levels until the late 1840s, after a decade and a half of war. The war forever divided El Salvador from Guatemala, and by 1839, El Salvador had officially seceded. It had not begun its era of independence with much luck, but the tiny nation strove ahead nonetheless.

CREATING A NATION

Independence from the rest of Central America did not bode well for El Salvador. Conflicts both internal and external continued unabated and its economic base shifted dramatically from indigo to coffee along with the shift to liberal policies by the 1880s. The new nation of El Salvador would continue to do battle with competing interests both within and outside its border. A central feature of El Salvador's national period was its Conservative-Liberal rivalry in the political arena, which had already boiled over many times during conflicts before independence, as demonstrated above. Interregional conflict also erupted frequently. Between 1841 and 1890, El Salvador fought with Guatemala five times, Honduras four times, and Nicaragua once. This volume of conflict was added to the 13 military coups that replaced the federal government during this period.

The conflicts from within fit in well with the increasing militarism of Salvadoran political culture throughout the nineteenth century despite the forward-looking politicians whose "goal of improving everything" (according to a July 30, 1859 editorial in *La Gaceta*) was interrupted frequently by armed conflict. From the beginning, security was the top priority of law makers who passed legislation expanding and refining police powers and security structures in 1825, 1843, 1848, 1854, 1855, 1868, 1889, and 1911. This last year witnessed the transition of the rural police into the Guardia Nacional (National Guard), which became notorious later in the twentieth century for its role in the repressive state apparatus that tortured and murdered thousands of Salvadorans. Military legislation increasingly expanded, with 30 legal stipulations providing for a more professionalized military between 1839 and 1858 alone.

An interesting comparison to make here is with the early national foundations of Costa Rica, one of El Salvador's close neighbors to the south. Costa Rica has no history of militarism. Not one of its presidents has been a military leader. There have been no violent overthrows of their government, and the one civil war that took place there in April of 1948 caused such distress with the role of violence in political affairs that the nation's leadership decided to abolish its national army. Unlike El Salvador, instead of increasing the role of the military in response to danger, Costa Rica demilitarized and began to rely on diplomacy and international organizations for support in the face of security pressures. El Salvador's beginnings were militaristic and only increased in this fashion throughout the century and a half that paved the road to the all-out civil war of the 1980s. The police and military forces received the most resources and funding, and thus, the most attention. Their presence did not reduce political violence but instead increased it, nor did it inhibit the rising levels of criminal activity in the countryside and the cities in the nineteenth, twentieth, or twenty-first centuries.

Political leadership has always presented a dilemma for El Salvador for several reasons. The nation has sought strong executives to control the country. This has caused many leaders to rely on military rather than civil political strength. The chaos surrounding the initial years of Central American independence led straight to this problem, and the country is only recently beginning to settle into a normal political flow, relatively untainted by military strength. The nation's first president, Juan Lindo (1790–1857), was a Honduran national who led El Salvador from 1841–1842, later becoming president of Honduras from 1847–1852. He had a mixed political history that would not favor Salvadoran autonomy, as he originally pushed for Central American incorporation into the Empire of Mexico under Agustin de Iturbide in the 1820s. Only when he fortuitously sought political office in El Salvador on the eve of Salvadoran independence from the Federal Republic of Central America did he gain a foothold that would allow him access to the leadership of the new country. By 1841, the same year of independence, he was elected president and immediately set forth plans to create better education in the country, including the opening of the University of El Salvador and a near-universal education platform.

After leaving the presidency in El Salvador, Lindo went on to lead Honduras, where he also initiated educational reforms and established an alliance with El Salvador for the joint invasion of Guatemala. Lindo's Honduran forces along with Salvadoran President Doroteo Vasconcelos's (1848–1851) Salvadorans invaded Guatemala in 1851 to vanquish Rafael Carrera (1839–1865) and were defeated. Lindo's legacy, although small, established for the state the value of providing education to the masses, albeit unequally. His followers would vary considerably, ranging from the undistinguished to the increasingly more significant. For example, the next presidency under José Escolástico Marín lasted all but three months in 1842, while his successor, Juan José Guzmán lasted two years from 1842–1844. It should also be kept in mind that El Salvador's presidential history is filled with interim leaders without the title of president who served briefly until more suitable leaders came along.

Guzmán's successor, General Francisco Malespín, only served from May 1844 to February 1845, but played a significant role in raising an army to put down an armed uprising. He immediately decreed that all males between 16 and 40 be prepared to put down the rebellion and set in motion a tighter infrastructure to carry out such measures in the future. However, less than a year into his presidency, he was forced to flee to Honduras where he was given asylum by the president of Honduras, Coronado Chavez, in March 1845. A year later, General Malespín was shot and killed in combat in Sonsonate Province as he attempted to retake power in El Salvador. His successor, General Fermin Palacios, served in an interim capacity and moderator role in between the forces of Malespín and his opponent, the Bishop Dr. Jorge Viteri y Ungo.

Palacios would end up serving as president technically for only a brief period in 1846, after handing over power to General Joaquin Guzman in 1845 in his capacity as a Senator. Such was the political environment in El Salvador during its infancy as a republic.

During this period, turmoil surrounded the political establishment as coups and countercoups took place. For example, President Malespín placed his vice president, Costa Rican born General Joaquin Guzman in command of the country in 1845 while Malespín fought the liberal regime of Nicaragua, resulting in Guzman's overthrow of his presidency. The following year, Bishop Viteri y Ungo successfully pushed liberal President Eugenio Aguilar out of office briefly, only to see him return due to popular pressure.

The next president, Eugenio Aguilar, began his political ascent in 1839 as the mayor of San Salvador, quickly rising through the political ranks in the 1840s by serving as the Surgeon General of the Army and later as the president of the National University. In February of 1846 he was handed the presidency by Senator Fermin Palacios. He is well known for actions such as expelling Bishop Viteri y Ungo from El Salvador for his complicity in rebellion against the government. His rule lasted until 1848, when elections brought his successor Doroteo Vasconcelos to the presidency.

President Vasconcelos's political career began at an early age, when El Salvador was yet to achieve true independence. When a civil war broke out in 1828, Vasconcelos was 25 years old and was granted the position of general minister of the state. Two years later he was made president of the Federal Congress. He later became chief politician (Jefe Politico) in 1836, and eventually left El Salvador for Europe for three years, returning for the elections of 1847, which he won. He served from 1848–1851. While not his immediate successor due to a brief interim presidency by Jose Felix Quiros, Francisco Dueñas took over later in 1851 and served three terms inconsecutively (1851–1852, 1852–1854, 1863–1871). Dueñas would play a significant role in Salvadoran politics for over three decades, being elected to Congress in 1837, and rapidly rising within the political scene to eventually take the presidency as the country continued to battle the chaos of the postindependence era, in addition to leading the country for three presidential terms.

Honduran born Jose Maria San Martin served as president from 1854–1856. He had technically spent one day as president in January of 1852 only to step down immediately in favor of Dueñas. As president, San Martin devoted his time to several creative projects such as the opening of the National University in San Vicente to complement the main campus in San Salvador and the founding of Nueva San Salvador after the old San Salvador had largely been destroyed by the great earthquake of 1854. After stepping down in 1856, San Martin served as senator, minister of Hacienda and War, and commander general of the army. It was this last assignment that led to his untimely death due to cholera, which resulted from battles in Nicaragua against the American filibuster William Walker. Rafael Campo became the next president after the Republican party placed him on the ballot against his will in 1856. Right away he set to work on rebuilding San Salvador and working together with other Central American nations to expel the American filibusters. His successor, Miguel Santín del Castillo served from 1858–1859 before handing over power to Gerardo Barrios, who would become the most beloved president of the Salvadoran military establishment for years to come.

The era of Gerardo Barrios (1859–1863) signaled the escalation of the role of the military in most aspects of Salvadoran life. Barrios professionalized and modernized the Salvadoran military, bringing in military uniforms and instructors from other militarized countries such as France and Colombia. He was known for extending El Salvador's foreign relations with many countries in a positive way as well, while also promoting jingoism through spreading fears about the constant threat of enemies infiltrating the country's social and political fabric. Barrios was somewhat of a positivist along the lines of other European-minded Latin American leaders of the latter half of the nineteenth century that sought to modernize their poor nations through immigration, export-led growth, and scientific principles of government along with the notions of order and progress.

Barrios especially had something in common with the great Argentine positivist and future president Domingo Faustino Sarmiento, who traveled to the United States in 1848–1849. Sarmiento witnessed the immense growth of the United States and wrote a 200-page letter back home to his countrymen extolling the country's virtues. Barrios instead went to Europe and wrote back in 1853 with explanations of how his trip inspired him to remake El Salvador along European lines. As with Sarmiento, Barrios represented the Salvadoran elites who chose to select only the aspects of nineteenth-century liberalism that benefited their class, while ignoring the type of social progress sought after by the west. They saw their future as based on material progress for themselves, and this further promoted the socioeconomic dichotomy between the wealthy minority and the poor majority. The positivist line of thinking solidified and entrenched the future Salvadoran elite values of preserving a landed elite that controlled the breadth of the country's resources. The power struggles of the initial decades of independence did not yield a freer, more pluralistic society, but instead led to the validation of a more hierarchical political system that in some ways returned the country to its feudalistic roots. This elite had little interest in fomenting a democratic citizenry that participated with any degree of agency in the organization of the country. Instead, it suited them perfectly to have a hierarchical oligarchy that controlled the government and the means of production that kept a largely ignorant majority well below them as an essential element in the equation. For example, in 1807, 76.5 percent of the male labor force dedicated itself to agricultural employment, and in 1858 that number had climbed to over 80 percent and in some cases close to 90 percent in places such as La Paz, Sonsonate, Cuscatlán, and Santa Ana.

Barrios's allegiance to elite sectors within the country runs parallel to many other leaders in the country's history with similar backgrounds. Although born in El Salvador somewhere in the department of San Miguel in 1813, his parents were Jose Maria Barrios and Margarita Cisneros Avila, and whose parents were each Spanish. His own parents possessed a great deal of land, as was typical of the upper class, where they grew crops such as indigo, coffee, cacao, and others, upon which the family grew wealthy. He had a reputation for wearing flashy uniforms, being close to his friends, speaking quietly, and living for his military service above all else. In fact, although he began his political career through nonviolent means, his star rose with military exploits during the years following Central American independence. However, as we have seen, those were formative years for the future of El Salvador that led the country into further political conflict and entrenched militarism.

By two years into Barrios's presidency, although the prospects for the country's future were not as bright as many others in Latin America, the country had made several strides forward in the areas of law and education. For example, in 1855, Isidro Menendez was called upon to create The Code of Commerce as a series of tomes dedicated to standardizing economic laws. By 1857, standard civil and criminal codes were enacted, and by 1860, so were penal and civil codes that were based on Spanish and Chilean foundations. In addition, after being aggravated by British economic blockades in 1842, 1843, 1844, 1849, and 1850, El Salvador established trade and peace treaties with other Central American countries, as well as Mexico, the United States, Belgium, Prussia, France, England, and Spain between 1849–1865, increasingly signaling that it was headed toward positivism and liberalism.

Barrios's tenure as president for four years paved the way for his successor, Francisco Dueñas, who served from 1863–1871. During the Barrios era, Dueñas went into exile and allied himself with a fellow conservative, the Guatemalan strongman, Rafael Carrera (1839–1865). Carrera and Barrios had a long-standing hostility toward one another that Barrios exacerbated with his call for the reunification of the Central American Union, to which Carrera responded by invading El Salvador and occupying Santa Ana and San Salvador in 1863. This action drove the president out of power, and Salvadoran conservatives placed Dueñas in power. Once in power, the new leader approved a new, more conservative constitution more in line with his own interests dating back to his early political career when he promoted the church as a fundamental institution of society. This was fundamentally opposed by the liberals who sought to abandon colonial institutions. He also built the National Palace in San Salvador and promoted coffee cultivation through credits and infrastructure improvements for large scale export of this crop that eventually became the backbone of the Salvadoran economy. Dueñas is especially known for widespread repression against his opponents, chief among them Barrios, who was executed after an abortive uprising in 1865. In 1871, Mariscal Santiago Gonzalez overthrew him in a liberal coup that drove Dueñas to the United States, where he spent the rest of his days.

Gonzalez, a Guatemalan by birth, would remain as president until 1876. Originally a Guatemalan liberal exiled to El Salvador in the 1850s, Gonzalez took advantage of various opportunities to serve the Salvadoran liberal party, and served as president of the legislature from 1862–1863 under Barrios. He served as military commander of the forces at Santa Ana when Carrera took over the country in 1863, and the Dueñas administration awarded him the position of Minister of War, where he oversaw the execution orders against Barrios. After overthrowing Dueñas in 1871, Gonzalez enacted several important liberal reforms that reduced the power of Church. He is also known for increasing the role of the military, improving the officers' academy, and naming it the Escuela Politecnica in 1871. This was also the year in which all males between 18 and 50 were forced to join the militia under order of the president. By 1880, there were 20,000 professional soldiers in El Salvador, with inequality seen in all of its structures: top officers earned wages 13 times that of soldiers, and soldiers mostly came from the peasantry.

EDUCATION

It is important to evaluate the immediate postindependence era through a system of variables. One way can be the political culture illustrated above. Another is the economy, and another is education, to which we turn now. Immediately after Central American independence, the federation followed the educational model developed by Englishmen Joseph Lancaster and Andrew Bell in which upper level students taught lower level students under a teacher's supervision. This became a widespread practice across Latin America, indicating another aspect of outside influence over a fundamental institution of the new country, such as was the case with the military in the latter half of the century and continuing on until the present. Jose Coelho of Brazil was the first Lancasterian teacher to organize schooling under this rubric in El Salvador in 1832. He opened the La Aurora de El Salvador and this served as the foundation of the nation's premier teaching school that finally opened in 1858. Being from Brazil, Coelho also knew a great deal about coffee growing and thus influenced its entrance into El Salvador.

The growth of schools has always been relatively slow going in El Salvador. There were only 6,696 students in the entire country in 1850 out of a population of 372,815. This number grew eventually to 29,427 by 1892 when the population had grown to 703,000 and education spending had grown 41 times from 1846–1892. By then, the educational system had become thoroughly professionalized and much more entrenched within society. Still, the economy and security were of higher importance than education, which was viewed more as a luxury than a necessity. This can be gleaned from the fact that schools opened and closed quite frequently and elite sectors had higher education access by several orders of magnitude. Instead, labor needs for commerce, public works, military and police service, and agriculture were deemed to be much higher priorities by governmental planners.

A quick comparison to Costa Rica is an apt exercise here. For example, Costa Rica spent up to 25 percent of its funds on education by the 1880s while El Salvador only scraped by with 5 percent. Costa Rica's military spending was always small and it would continue to decline after its 1948 civil war that was almost immediately followed by the abolition of the army by revolutionary leader Jose "Pepe" Figures. By contrast, El Salvador only increased its spending even as education became more important to most other developing countries. For example, average military spending was 27 percent in El Salvador during peace time, and up to 50 percent during war time. However, education has been somewhat of a priority since the beginning of the republic when the first president, Juan Lindo decided to found the University of el Colegio de la Asuncion in 1841. Unfortunately, an earthquake destroyed it in 1854 and the government failed in finding enough competent professors in El Salvador and instead sought them from Europe. By 1888, the higher education system was floundering with only 180 students at the university and only 528 citizens had diplomas in the entire country. Other statistics in this regard are indeed staggering for 1888, with a 1:32 ratio for students in primary school, 1:530 in secondary school, and 1:3,830 in higher education.

This matters especially because the opening and ever-expanding international economy could only be sufficiently exploited by Salvadorans with educational backgrounds that would allow them to tap into this growing network. With such a limited access to education, and with higher education confined entirely to the elites, the colonially entrenched system of inequality based on race (primarily white and secondarily ladino, but never Indian) and family background only continued with the postcolonial national period of liberalism of the late nineteenth century.

ECONOMY

As liberal economic ideals took hold in El Salvador, the government promoted infrastructure improvements and developments in order to support increased trade. They built and improved roads between the major cities and the ports such as those running between Santa Ana and San Salvador and San

Miguel and between these and the coastal cities of Acajutla, La Libertad, and La Union, respectively. However, problems such as heavy rains, war, and bandits made it difficult at times, and these hindrances to development became cause for the heavier trafficked areas to be monitored more closely by government officials and police in particular. These problems still persist in modern El Salvador.

The government also began large scale shifts in land tenure policies with the rise of positivism. By the 1850s, a proactive effort was made to sell off public lands, often under Indian control merely for subsistence agricultural purposes, in order to pave the way toward land privatization. The result was the maximum usage of land for the cultivation of export commodities such as coffee and indigo. In fact, after 1880, the government divided up and sold communally held ejidos and other types of communal holdings so that large haciendas and fincas stood as the dominant forms of land holding by the end of the nineteenth century, just as they had at the end of the sixteenth, seventeenth, and eighteenth centuries. The achievement of independence from Spain signaled very little positive change in the area of progressive land reform.

The dismantlement of the ejido system was not met with universal enthusiasm. In fact, there was dissent in several areas, chief among them the Indians who suffered from this action. After the 1871 overthrow of the conservative Dueñas government, the liberal Gonzalez government became more active in breaking up the ejidos and communal property, which formed much of the background of the conflicts that sprang up in and around Izalco from 1872 to 1898.

5

Coffee and Militarization, 1871–1932

The period between 1871 and 1932 witnessed a tremendous shift in Salvadoran society. El Salvador changed from indigo producer to coffee producer. El Salvador became more liberal economically, yet less democratic, more militarized, and thus more violent. At the same time, there were reformers, but they tended toward increasing the consolidation of power into the hands of the elite and away from the majority of the population. Although we can not generalize completely by asserting that the status quo was preserved entirely, for there were minor changes, this era more than anything else entrenched the coffee oligarchy that would rule El Salvador for over a century. Its interests were protected above all else, and whenever common Salvadorans called for change, their interests mattered not.

The six-decade history that unfolds herein begins with land-based Indian revolts in Izalco, which began in the 1870s. An interesting footnote of U.S.-Salvadoran relations history is that the Military History Museum in San Salvador has at least 100 U.S.-made weapons on display, the earliest of which dates back to 1872. The fact that there are at least 99 other U.S. weapons on display that chart consistent U.S. military assistance to the Salvadoran governments, even as they carried out massive repression against their populations, demonstrates the deep and long-lasting roots of U.S. connections to the Salvadoran military/elite alliance. However, it must be noted that despite this connection, the United States has had much less economic influence in the country due to the presence of the entrenched coffee oligarchy (the Fourteen Families), whose ascendancy dates back to this very period in the second half of the nineteenth century.

This in itself helps us understand that U.S. interests in El Salvador were much less concerned with making money as they were with the generalized interests among states to aid one's allies. In the Salvadoran-U.S. case, we see a 138-year history of U.S. military aid to a government that has enjoyed only a two-decade history of democracy. While the display of the military's own museum does not explain the entire nature of U.S.-Salvadoran relations, it does help us to comprehend at least one specific thing: that the only connections that have existed between our two governments have been confined to officialdom, which has automatically excluded the voices of the downtrodden and disenfranchised masses of El Salvador. This system of connections has a built-in obstacle to understanding reality on the ground from the U.S. perspective. That is, whenever revolts on the part of the antidictatorial forces took place in El Salvador, the government of the United States had only the government of El Salvador to provide the reality of the situation, thus skewing the reality of history. As a result, Indian uprisings were put down with the help of U.S. weaponry supplied to the Salvadoran government, as would future uprisings for over a century afterward.

REVOLTS IN IZALCO

Many have observed that the break up of Indian communal lands in the late nineteenth century caused a series of revolts against government officials who partitioned the lands and the landowners who benefited. This notion has recently been challenged in light of more in depth investigation into the inner workings of community relationships between classes and races. However, the issue of land control itself is still the central problem the locals around Izalco dealt with at the time, and the struggles they endured are indicative of how the liberal administrations' policies that favored land consolidation for the purposes of supporting the growth of the coffee export sector bore fruit. A significant part of this new evidence is that there were in fact well-to-do Indians who owned large parcels of land that yielded high profits during this period. These Indians used communal lands for coffee and sugar production for commercial purposes, which conflicted with those indigenous peoples set on maintaining the basic subsistence agricultural practices associated with their traditional way of life. This represented a deep source of conflict within the very communities that would need solidarity as a single unit in order to not be consumed by the dominant ladino community.

The Salvadoran government's laws eliminating collectively held lands in 1881 and 1882 precipitated some of the future crises, despite the first uprisings of the 1870s, which resulted from government repression and corruption. However, it only stood to reason that the law's effect extended as far as the government was willing to enforce this edict. There were also short-lived uprisings in 1885 and 1894, but the most significant one occurred in 1898. This was largely based on disgruntled Indians angry with the decision making of judges who divided their land. The punishment meted out by the attackers was to sever the hands of these judges in order to destroy the objects that had provided the measurements used to divide these lands.

Events such as the uprising did more in favor of lifting the dominant elite position within Salvadoran society than it hindered it, namely because the uprising was crushed. The country was also experiencing the nature of the international economic opening going on at the time. Several factors contributed toward this for Salvadorans around mid-century: the construction of railroads in Panama, the California gold rush, the American Civil War, and especially the shift from indigo to coffee as the top Salvadoran export commodity. The latter occurrence led to such problems as the marginalization of subsistence agriculture in the country due to the fact that most of the arable land became dedicated to export agriculture due to the rising demand of coffee on the world market.

To understand the magnitude of this increase from mid-century to the end, consider that in 1855, a population of 394,000 exported a total of 765,324 pesos worth of goods, while in 1892, 703,000 people exported close to 7 million pesos worth of goods. This represented a five-fold per capita increase in exports, not unlike that experienced in places like Mexico and Argentina, whose exports increased up to nine-fold in the latter half of the century due to positivist principles as well. How did this happen so quickly in El Salvador? As transportation costs went down in the nineteenth century due to enhanced mechanization and improved efficiency techniques in assembly procedures, and so forth, the incentive to export increased in tandem. This along with the rising demand for coffee during the California gold rush helped to ease the transition from indigo to coffee, which began in 1855. By 1892, coffee exports were 80 percent of the total exports for all of El Salvador.

This occurred just as another precipitous historical process was being set into motion in the United States. A small cotton boom took place in El Salvador in reaction to the loss of American cotton production during the Civil War, which caused an increase in demand and prices in England, whose industrial production demanded cotton for textiles. Cotton is still an important export product in El Salvador today. The cotton boom took the country by surprise, as indigo had almost totally dominated the Salvadoran economy for the entire colonial period and into the initial decades of the national period. In fact, it was the indigo boom in 1610 through 1630 that initially opened El Salvador to world trade and the crop took off afterward under the repartimiento system. By 1855, it was over 86 percent of El Salvador's exports, with hides, tobacco, balsam, and other minor products far behind. The 1870s witnessed a rival in coffee.

The shift from indigo to coffee had several underlying causes. Shipping problems with the colonial product became clear in the pre-1850s era, when indigo bound for England had to either go overland through Belize or around Cape Horn first, each of which lasted many months and incurred sometimes prohibitively high costs. Steamship services that transported people and goods from Central America to California began in 1854 with the demands coming from people heading to California for the gold rush that had begun in 1848. Once steamship service was established to Panama and goods could be transported across the isthmus via the railroads there by 1855 transportation time was cut in half, reducing overall transportation costs considerably.

This process then accelerated the liberal economic notion of export-led growth in El Salvador to a level never seen before, albeit on a scale that paled by comparison to Mexico and Argentina, for example, which attracted higher foreign investments and possessed the tools for economic diversification. This trend toward export-led growth had some residual effects such as the marginalization of indigenous wares such as cotton and food in favor of exporting coffee for the importation of foreign goods, such as cotton and textiles, each being items El Salvador had the ability to produce for themselves, and luxury items, a process already set in motion during the colonial era but greatly accelerated at the end of the nineteenth century.

Taken as a whole, the transition to coffee away from indigo was quite gradual, with indigo exports still at one million pounds in the last years of the nineteenth century. In fact, coffee never pushed indigo out entirely or even by its own volition. The eventual loss of the indigo market was more a result of the gradual introduction of synthetic dyes into the world dye market. This occurred at the same time as coffee received more and more investment. The government sold uncultivated land to coffee producers at cheap prices to increase the incentive for coffee production as well. But why choose coffee over indigo? By one estimate, it may have been the result of individual rational economic choices by entrepreneurs weighing the costs between different commodities and taking advantage of the drop in transportation costs for coffee during the 1850s and 1860s more so than they did for indigo. The demand for indigo was still high during this period; however, the introduction of synthetic dyes also introduced unwanted competition, which drove down incentives for production along with market prices. The shift to coffee also altered the economic landscape of the country, with indigo formerly produced mostly in the east in San Miguel and San Vicente and coffee produced in the center and west. Thus, cities like Santa Ana, Ahuachapan, and Sonsonate gained in importance with the coffee boom. All together, these three alone had over three million coffee trees in 1857, all of which were ready to produce within the coming years.

El Salvador's economic place in the world is understood by economists in terms of the small country phenomenon. Small countries economically operate at the whims of larger countries mostly outside of their own control, which can have positive and/or negative consequences. For example, El Salvador profited both from the Panama railroad route (and later, the Canal that opened in 1914) as well as the increase in trade along the Pacific Coast, such as with the California gold rush. The Salvadoran government only increased the trends set in motion by the Spanish colonial authorities profiting from the indigo trade during the colonial period. The new elites subsidized the coffee industry just like the colonial elites had subsidized indigo, and all for their own profit by providing inexpensive land, building and improving roads and ports, and in subsidizing shipping costs by paying the steamers operating with the Panama Railroad Company. All of this spelled great incentives for coffee production and a lack of incentive for other production.

LIBERALISM TAKES HOLD
AND FALLS, 1871–1932

The following years represented a liberal period in Salvadoran politics in which the main political divisions were among liberal minded leaders. These leaders sometimes disagreed about the extent to which liberalism would be followed, but they were on the same page about economic policies whereby the state supported growth but did not hinder it. The government's role was seen as providing infrastructure that facilitated trade by building roads, railways, encouraging foreign investment and immigration, and generally doing whatever was necessary to support the export of high volumes of coffee. What began as an era of economic promise with the rise of liberal ideals in 1871, ended with the worst era of bloodshed the country had ever seen with *La Matanza* that killed between 10,000 and 30,000 people. At the same time, El Salvador became the biggest proponent of the reunification of Central America, but these efforts failed.

This was an era of elections as well as coups, but presidents tended to serve longer terms than in the first four decades of independence. The first president of this era was Mariscal Santiago Gonzalez (1871–1876), a liberal leader who overthrew Francisco Dueñas in 1871, the last conservative president for the next six decades. Gonzalez lasted until 1876, during which time he became known for promoting the reunification of Central America with agreements signed with Guatemala, Honduras, and Costa Rica in 1872 and a meeting held in 1876 in which Nicaragua, Guatemala, El Salvador, Honduras, and Costa Rica all pushed for the restoration of the union.

A change of power took place in February 1876 with the presidency shifting to Andres Valle for three months until Dr. Rafael Zaldívar (1876–1885) claimed power for the next nine years. President Zaldívar had a long-running career as a politician and academic as well as a physician prior to his presidential aspirations. He is best known for following ideals best embodied by Mexican politicians such as Benito Juarez and Porfirio Diaz. He went much further than they did in marginalizing the *ejido* communities than did Juarez, but he was also never the champion of democracy that Juarez was to Mexico. In fact, he eliminated the *ejido* and communal land systems in El Salvador as a means of consolidating liberal economic principals of export-led agriculture for capitalist growth. Zaldívar eventually ran into problems with his neighbor, the long-lasting liberal president Justo Rufino Barrios (1873–1885), who decided to invade El Salvador in 1885 in a fateful move that ended with Barrios's death. The United States even sent the naval ship USS *Wachusett* down to Central America during the war for fear that unrest would threaten U.S. businesses in Nicaragua, Guatemala, and El Salvador due to Barrios's threat to sabotage American-owned telegraph lines in El Salvador.

Shortly after the Guatemalan army's retreat, Zaldívar stepped down as president and Francisco Menendez (1885–1890) took his place. Menendez made a name for himself through the approval of the 1886 constitution that lasted until 1939, after seven constitutions had been written to that point since independence. Menendez's overthrow in 1890 by Carlos Ezeta (1890–1894) led to Ezeta's four-year reign, setting in motion a series of coup attempts that finally halted in 1903 with an electoral system that paralleled Mexico's Institutional Revolutionary Party (PRI) for 71 years in the twentieth century. Although lasting for a much shorter period of time than the PRI later in the century, each president would select his successor who would then be elected under the guise of democratic elections. The 1890s also witnessed efforts led by El Salvador to reunify Central America, only to end by 1898.

The culture of violence was growing during this time as well. As a country still in its formative years in many ways, the creation of a state apparatus that served at the whims of the elite and the military thus depended on an unequal relationship between itself and the poor majority, which often times responded with violence in kind. For example, landowners who treated their peasant workers unfairly through low wages and cruel treatment elicited negative reactions from their employees who would then threaten their masters with bodily harm. The landowners would then pay guards to threaten the peasantry in turn, thus perpetuating a cycle of action and reaction based on the use of force to grease the wheels of interaction. This environment was the least conducive to the creation of democracy in a small, feudalistic, poor country.

However, violence was by no means limited to class conflict. In fact, it was quite common to hear of violence used between wealthy men who hired their own workers to fight against each other on the landowners' behalf. This was also true of the poor sectors themselves, who traded violence in their own disputes. The leaders of the country were no better, as there were exactly 58 presidencies between 1841 and 1898. Their example merely represented what was going on across the country. From the national level, the presidents learned that to control the rest of the country, they needed allegiance at the local levels through leaders that were amenable to the president's interests and therefore, to the military and the oligarchy as well. Therefore, the local leadership would use violence to repress the very people they were sworn to represent and defend, upon the orders of the national leadership. An example of this was the consistent use of police and military units to force peasants to work on haciendas or give up land to wealthier owners for the purposes of enriching the already rich and powerful classes.

THE NEW CENTURY

The twentieth century dawned over El Salvador with the promise of a new day in old clothing. The militarism of the past remained while the progress of the future continued through the sustained and growing promotion of the coffee industry that placed El Salvador on the map. Coffee played a central role in politics as it was the economic lifeblood of the country. The century's first president carried over from the previous century. General Tomas Regalado (1898–1903) had a history of high level leadership both within the military and the government. In particular he was known for participating in the overthrow of the Ezeta government in 1894 and later led the overthrow of Gutierrez in 1898. Regalado was killed in Guatemala in 1906, during which time his successor, General Pedro Jose Escalon (1903–1907) was in the process of developing the national image through such public projects as the inauguration of the construction of the National Palace, the National Theater, and the National Museum. General Fernando Figueroa (1907–1911), according to the scant information available, appears to have had an uneventful presidency save for experiencing criticism from opposition movements in the west of the country.

A significant event took place in 1912 with the assassination of President Manuel Enrique Araujo (1911–1912). Araujo represented a partial break with the past, having established the first workers' protection laws during his short presidency. After his death, Carlos Melendez took power until 1919, after which his brother Jorge served until 1923 and then Jorge's brother-in-law, Alfonso Quiñonez Molina, served until 1927. A notable feature of the era from 1912–1927 is the relative stability of the political situation in El Salvador, which was preserved by massive suppression of dissidence and oppression against the poor majority. However, things changed briefly for the better with Molina's chosen successor, Pio Romero Bosque (1927–1931), who tried to placate both the wealthy and the poor to a degree. For example, he isolated himself from the previous dynastic rulers and even promoted a free and fair presidential election at the conclusion of his own. It was the last El Salvador would see by many standards until close to the end of the century.

COFFEE, LAND DISTRIBUTION, AND POLITICS

As the presidencies were intimately linked to coffee interests, it seems fitting to take a moment to discuss how coffee affected all aspects of life in El Salvador at the beginning of the century. For example, although there are many variations in the sizes of coffee plots, ranging from just under a few acres to several square miles, the majority of the coffee lands have always been in the hands of large holders. Much of this consolidation took place during the liberalization period of 1880–1912 in which small owners were forced to sell to wealthier owners. One major reason for this is that coffee production is less conducive to the poor farmer who lives hand to mouth. This has to do among other things with the growing cycle itself: coffee plants take five years to mature before they can yield a crop, which means that small farmers risk a considerable amount by depending too heavily on coffee and they therefore tend to divide their time and effort between food crops for subsistence and coffee for market. This makes for an ideal situation for wealthier producers who can afford to purchase floundering coffee enterprises from poor farmers looking for a quick sale during hard times. The result was a flood of sales of inexpensive, small plots of land that went into the hands of the landowning elite.

The plantation itself illustrated the impact of the coffee industry on many levels of life. A typical coffee plantation well into the twentieth century consisted of a poor work environment for the peasant who labored all day for an owner who provided only two meals plus a meager wage. Unions were strictly prohibited throughout most of the century as well, which severely limited the peasantry's ability to improve their lot. This occurred due to the power of the elites within politics, to state the obvious. For example, by 1895, most lawmakers made their living from coffee growing, and between the 1898 overthrow of General Tomas Regalado, and 1931 every president was a coffee grower. In addition, the great economic growth beginning with a boom in 1915 provided more power to the coffee oligarchy that was increasingly inclined to support politicians in line with them and likewise meant that the oligarchy had more funds with which to buy military and police support to pressure small holders into selling their lands.

In fact, revolutionaries who took up arms in 1932 mentioned the coffee-based economic system as the country's number one problem, citing the fact that the economy had been more diversified and less dependent before the shift away from indigo to coffee. This dependency was primarily a relationship that relied heavily on foreign capital, especially from the United States and Germany, which purchased a large proportion of the Salvadoran coffee crop. However, one important exception must be clarified in the case of the Salvadoran economy. The land and resources were not owned by foreign companies to the degree in which they were owned in the neighboring countries such as Honduras, Guatemala, Nicaragua, and Costa Rica. El Salvador had a sufficient number of wealthy landed elite to run affairs from within, and therefore companies such as Standard Fruit and United Fruit had very little influence there.

There were also significant landowner class distinctions in El Salvador at this time. There were *latifundistas* that dedicated their land to farming products for food consumption, and *terratenientes,* who dedicated their land to coffee, which gradually overtook the *latifundistas* in the twentieth century, with four-fifths of the land in the hands of several hundred coffee growing families. This high level of dependency meant that the Great Depression beginning in 1929 caused dramatic downfalls in incomes for the majority of the country's workers. As coffee is a luxury commodity, Americans and Germans chose not to purchase as much of the product during their own economic downturn and the Salvadorans suffered as a result. This suffering took on various forms, such as malnourishment, the necessity for mobility, the break up of families, and other problems.

By the time of the 1931 elections, the Left in El Salvador as well as Indian groups were ready for revolt. The Central American Workers Federation (COCA) with links to Guatemalans, Salvadorans, and Hondurans was formed in 1922 and contained a strong labor movement in El Salvador under the name of the Regional Federation of Workers of El Salvador (FRTS). By 1929, FRTS was consumed almost entirely by the mostly Marxist organization, the Latin American Syndical Confederation, and by 1930, the Communist Party in El Salvador was large enough to march 80,000 members and supporters through San Salvador on May Day.

It was El Salvador's national hero, Agustin Farabundo Martí, who led the dissident movement in those days. His Red Aid International (SRI) was led by Marxists, but did not contain a majority membership of Communists. The famous revolutionary Miguel Marmol also played a prominent role with Martí in fomenting rebellion. Martí actually made his way to the United States in 1928, eventually ending up in Nicaragua to join the rebellion led by that country's revolutionary martyr, Augusto Cesar Sandino. The two parted ways in Mexico the following year due to a difference of ideology, as Sandino was more a nationalist mostly seeking the expulsion of the U.S. Marines and a return to democracy, whereas Martí sought communist insurrection. Martí would have his opportunity three years later, only to have it crushed before it got off the ground.

Most of the work done by Martí and his followers centered on distributing political propaganda deemed a crime by the government in 1930. In fact, many hundreds of people were punished for breaking this law, either through imprisonment or worse and this became yet another factor legitimizing insurrection in the minds of the peasantry and labor classes. It was this action that led to the activism of Martí's SRI, who collected resources to assist the prisoners and their families and to draw attention to the mass imprisonment as a human rights issue.

THE ELECTION OF 1931

As the common Salvadorans began to agitate for change, so did top politicians. Arturo Araujo became the candidate of the new Salvadoran Labor Party that was in part modeled off Great Britain's party of the same name. Araujo had spent considerable time in Europe. With the help of the famous poet Alberto Masferrer, Araujo constructed a campaign platform calling for the promotion of his image as a people's candidate through the concept of *vitalismo. Vitalismo* signified the state's role in safeguarding everyone's right to the minimum necessities of life. Therefore, issues such as land reform and social welfare were first and foremost on his list of campaign elements. The election results placed Araujo in the lead but without a simple majority, which required the vote to be decided in the legislature, who selected Araujo as the undisputed winner.

The United States had worried about the possibility of unrest in El Salvador and therefore sent the USS *Sacramento* down to Nicaragua. One of Araujo's first decisions was to allow the minister of war, General Maximiliano Hernandez Martinez to be his vice president, a move that later proved costly. Soon Araujo's advisor Masferrer left his side just as labor unrest by the FRTS and Martí's SRI was on the rise. The end of Araujo's presidency came in December of 1931 when opposition officers took control of the city, at first even capturing vice president Martinez. Martinez was eventually placed in control himself, and he carried out the massacre of 1932 known simply as *La Matanza*. Araujo was driven into exile in Honduras.

Agustin Farabundo Martí had been in and out of El Salvador for years trying to build up momentum for his movement, finally returning for the last time in February 1931. He lasted one year until his execution in February 1932. 1931 was the year Martí became well known for rallying large parts of western El Salvador to the cause of revolution, in particular Indians that had found it difficult to ally themselves to ladinos in the past. Martí's rebellion was slated for late January 1932, but was stifled as a result of his arrest, along with the arrest of other plotters. The police discovered the details of the revolt and proceeded to carry out a state of siege regime in the west (San

Salvador, Ahuachapan, Santa Ana, La Libertad, Sonsonate, Chalatenango). The scheduled revolt for late January did take place, but it was much too small to succeed and the government forces were already prepared. The major fighting took place briefly in Juayua, a small coffee growing town just north of Sonsonate that had suffered greatly due to a recent collapse in coffee prices, as well as in other small towns.

The battle for Juayua placed the rebels in a light they would later regret. A radical involved with FRTS named Chico Sanchez led an armed group of 500 men in Juayua on the fateful night of January 22, 1932. The mostly Indian rebels ransacked the town for supplies and money and even murdered the town benefactor, Italian-born Emilio Redaelli. The rest of El Salvador heard of these events and was soon galvanized against the rebellion. The rebels then moved on to the city of Nahuizalco and others, leaving minor destruction in their path, yelling the slogan, "Viva Socorro Rojo!" or "Long Live Red Aid."

The rebels were eventually subdued and the resulting massacre of mostly Indian rebels and civilians in the west of El Salvador especially led to the deaths of 10,000–30,000 people in the days that followed. Despite the initial violence of the uprising, the military response can only be described as excessive in the extreme sense of the word. The stories of survivors resemble actions taken by the planet's most brutal regimes of the century. The testimony given by Dionisio Nerio, a man who lived through the massacre of both rebels and civilians around Nahuizalco illustrates this well. He stated that those men found by the military without a pass that distinguished friend from foe were rounded up at a local military outpost, where they were then taken out in groups of eight and shot. The rows of dead men were then put into a pit behind them, over and over again, as the bodies piled up. Dionisio Nerio was in one of these lines but was missed by the bullets meant for him and therefore was able to survive to tell his story. He asserts that 985 victims were shot that day alone. Considering the total number of civilians killed by the military during *La Matanza,* which wiped out much of the remaining Indian population, the small number of less than 100 people killed by the rebels pales by comparison.

The result of the rebellion was a heightened culture of fear of the government forces that lasted until 1992. Many of the surviving Indians resolved to eschew or hide their traditional culture in order to protect themselves from future persecution, indicating yet another level of destruction accomplished by the military. They knew that the government had targeted their fellow Pipils especially and therefore chose to blend in more as a result. This is quite different from the rest of Latin America, where the indigenous populations have more options for maintaining their integrity as cultural and ethnic groups.

Martí's execution had the immediate effect of signaling the end of the rebellion that had germinated for so many years before his capture. The government of General Martinez made sure the proceedings appeared perfectly legitimate by first having a trial and conviction before the execution. However, the following decades enhanced Martí's image to that of a revolutionary martyr in the eyes of the peasantry, working classes, and intellectuals, the evidence of which is best embodied in the name of the main umbrella guerrilla group of the 1980s, the Farabundo Martí National Liberation Front (FMLN). At the same time, General Martinez has became a villain to most and the savior of El Salvador to the elite and the military. Much of this has to do with distortions of the actual history that occurred in the wake of *La Matanza*. For example, while rumors persisted about the guerrillas receiving considerable support from communists abroad (which proved to be false), and there were spurious stories of communists killing hundreds of people as opposed to simply 100 or less, the military government also destroyed all records of their own role in the killings. Researchers have had to use other means to put the pieces together, most of which are understood now.

What also became known as a result of this massacre of civilians was the magnitude of the problem that existed in El Salvador as a result of the military-oligarchy alliance. The military was technically under civilian control according to the 1886 constitution, but a tacit arrangement existed whereby military leaders became president many times as long as the interests of the concentrated wealthy elite were protected. This mutual reinforcement made sure to keep any real dissident movement under wraps through repeated demonstrations of repression that had been in place for decades leading up to *La Matanza*. The following five decades saw the continuation of this system in large part until the next wave of mass repression culminated with the civil war of the 1980s.

And as with the 1980s, the United States weighed in on the side of the elites in 1932. The coffee industry had a lot to do with this because El Salvador had gone into debt to Great Britain during the drop in coffee prices after World War I, leaving the country at the mercy of foreigners to help them recover. United States banks offered up the capital to help the country out briefly while placing an American agent in charge of monitoring trade duties, which was seen quite negatively in El Salvador. This was quite a rarity in El Salvador, as opposed to the rest of Central America. El Salvador had a long history of relative independence from foreign ownership because the oligarchy preferred power to remain in their hands. And for the most part the United States stayed out of Salvadoran affairs, but with the rising Red scare in the Americas, the U.S. government admitted that Martinez had improved his image by putting down the rebellion so efficiently, and in 1934, the United States officially recognized his regime.

6

La Matanza and Beyond, 1932–1972

THE MARTINEZ REGIME, 1932–1944

With *La Matanza* fresh in everyone's minds, the battle for the future would be decided by the images portraying the meaning of the event itself. El Salvador would not pull itself out of the cloud of militarism in the least over the next four decades due to the absolute control over the levers of influence on the part of those elements with an interest in upholding the legitimacy of the widespread suppression of the impoverished majority that culminated with the orchestrated murder of some 10,000–30,000 people in 1932. The future of El Salvador was up for grabs only to the extent that sectors of the country were willing to risk everything to confront such a powerful force as the military-elite alliance that was so fundamental to the power structure of this unique little country so close to the most powerful nation on Earth.

The regime under the general who planned, carried out, and benefited the most from *La Matanza* lasted 12 years and solidified the military state in El Salvador. The popular opinion among the elite throughout most of this period followed the line of thinking that the political opening of 1931 led to a communist rebellion of epic proportions that was supported by foreign elements, and thus they viewed pluralism negatively and supported centralized militarism. The possibility that the rebels' concerns were legitimate never entered their collective consciousness, further illuminating the profound differences that have long existed in El Salvador, and which increasingly perpetuated themselves over the course of the twentieth century through political leadership being centered in the hands of a minority. General Maximiliano Hernandez Martinez understood the power he now held, and especially that this power rested largely on his credibility as someone perceived to have saved the fatherland from certain doom. Therefore, he used this clout to enhance the power of the military by continuing to promote fears about internal security threats. In addition, most of his cabinet ministers were military officials, which fomented an environment of compliance among his advisors. He also increased the government's role in the economy, and although he tried to protect elite interests, in the long run, his populist streak aimed at widening his base of support through minor reform programs led the elites to reject him eventually.

However, Martinez pleased the elites for a while, especially with measures that made them feel more secure. For example, Martinez began the institutionalization of the requirement that all residents carry a state-issued identification card on them at all times, known as a *cédula de vecindad.* This method began during *La Matanza* with predictable results, and was also required in Stalinist Russia, to name just one absolute dictatorship who utilized this technique of control. Political freedom was also severely curtailed under this regime, with the Communist Party declared illegal and the prohibition of all dissident literature enforced with the utmost strictness. However, at the same time, Martinez alienated members of the elite with vested interests in preserving the status quo, which meant the increasing socioeconomic dichotomization of society. Due to the depression of the 1930s, the coffee industry faced disastrous consequences, in particular for the smaller and medium producers. In response, Martinez declared a moratorium on debts and a 40 percent reduction in interest payments in order to cushion the blow of the economic downturn for these producers. He also created the Central Reserve Bank and the Mortgage Bank through the state apparatus in order to protect vulnerable owners from fluctuations in the world economy. While these moves initially made some elites nervous, they eventually proved to save the economy from short term disaster, and thus helped Martinez recover their support. By 1939, Martinez had a new constitution drawn up that gave the state an unprecedented role in controlling the economy, communication, and the media.

General Martinez was also known for mild efforts to alleviate poverty through land reform. However, the reform programs did very little to help the average peasant, with little efficiency or care going into solving the real people affected by poverty on the ground. At the same time, Martinez's popularity began to wane considerably after 1939 when civilian officials resigned in protest against his third presidential bid. They denounced Martinez for failing to alternate power consistently as outlined in the 1886 constitution. Eventually, the dictator lost support among the elites and middle class by wearing out the old story of the constant internal security threats posed by foreign supported communists, his lack of democratic aspirations, and his fledgling programs for the poor.

His downfall came in 1944 with a mass movement led by students in tandem with opponents among the elite, middle class, and military elements. The Salvadoran Democratic Action movement was created in opposition to Martinez in 1941 with Agustin Alfaro Moran, a well-known coffee grower and official within the coffee growing industry. An initial revolt on the part of disenchanted soldiers failed with heavy losses but triggered the uprising led by Democratic Action that led to Martinez's departure from office. In the days leading up to the overthrow there were accusations against Martinez claiming that he had concocted the idea of the communist rebellion of 1932 in order to justify *La Matanza* and as a result, his own rule. In addition, there was evidence that his supporters were conjuring up a similar action among students in 1944 in order to provoke a call for his return.

FOLLOWING IN MARTINEZ'S FOOTSTEPS, 1944–1960

The years following the overthrow of Martinez signaled a sea change in Salvadoran political life. Despite the fact that the outgoing dictator placed his own choice in the presidency (General Andres I. Menendez), pluralism regained its popularity briefly once Martinez left, keeping in mind that this was Salvadoran pluralism, meaning still in its infancy. For example, previously banned political groups such as the Communists were now allowed to operate, as was the group that pushed the hardest for Martinez's overthrow, Democratic Action, which now operated under the name Democratic Union Party (PUD). Elections were immediately scheduled to take place during the summer of 1944.

The two main parties vying for control were of the same ilk as the competing forces during the last years of the Martinez dictatorship. The PUD supported Arturo Romero, a leader of the anti-Martinez opposition movement leading up to his ouster, while former supporters of the fallen dictator created the Unification Social Democratic Party (PUSD) and ran General Salvador Castañeda Castro. The PUD eventually expanded and consumed more political actors, becoming the United Democratic Front (FUD). Of course, this democratic opening quickly closed shut with the military overthrow of the Menendez government by Colonel Osmin Aguirre y Salinas that same year, driving his political opponents out of the country and into the jails. The FUD then launched an invasion force of 2,000 fighters against Aguirre from Guatemala, only to be quashed with mass casualties. The Castañeda regime was confirmed in January of 1945, and he too was overthrown in 1948 after assuming he could increase his term by two years. The forces that rebelled were a revolutionary movement led by high ranking officers who then incorporated civilians into their new Revolutionary Governing Council. However, even though the new group of leaders had revolutionary ideals (indeed, this movement is referred to as "The Revolution of 1948"), they were still caught up in the process of militarization that had been in the making since the inception of El Salvador as a republic, and which had been consolidated under the Martinez military apparatus.

Between 1948 and 1972, the military establishment tried to be the only governing force in the country, which led them to pretend to incorporate as many societal elements as possible into their fray. The problem lay in their inability to do so mostly due to their main allegiance to the elite class, whom they also failed to fully satisfy. Instead of seeking to alleviate the poor conditions of the majority of the country, they relied on the tried and true method of throwing the proverbial bone down the socioeconomic ladder hoping to placate the sentiments of those who had supported revolutionary radicalism in the past. The military sought out people who would maintain their authority across the country. In the place of creating programs that responded to the problems of the rural poor population, the military sought the support of squads that protected the oligarchy through the use of violence and intimidation, thus resulting in groups such as the Democratic Nationalist Organization (ORDEN). The public became even less enamored with the military as a legitimate governing force because of this and the true growth of democratic values among the educated and poor classes surged in reaction to these militaristic measures all the way until the 1972 election. And because the doors to change were consistently slammed shut, after 1972, these sentiments turned to armed insurrection as the only option for enacting change. When taking a close look at Salvadoran history, it becomes clear how the foundations for opposition to democracy had become so fully entrenched within the military and oligarchy that all possibilities for true pluralism had been completely closed long ago.

However, the chief executives continued to pretend that democracy reigned supreme. For example, in 1950, Oscar Osorio (1950–1956) took office and instituted a new constitution that gave the government the right to intervene at will in the economy. This was seen as both good and bad, depending on which side one was on. For example, the state used tax revenues to develop the growth of infrastructure aimed at facilitating trade, such as the building of roads, electric connections, ports, and railroads, while culling funds for low cost subsidized housing. The new political party that managed this platform was the Revolutionary Party of Democratic Unification (PRUD). PRUD resembled the corporatist ideology of Mexico's Institutional Revolutionary Party (PRI) whereby the party portrayed itself as incorporating all political elements of the country under one umbrella organization that represented the interests of everyone. Unlike the PRI, however, the reforms carried out under the PRUD fell far short of revolutionary. In Mexico, the PRI redistributed tens of millions of acres of land previously in the hands of elites prior to the Mexican Revolution (1910–1920), and set up support for these new farmers in the form of low-interest loans and subsidies managed by the state. It is a given that this reform program did not work well for many Mexicans; however, the PRI was able to maintain a semblance of legitimacy in the eyes of the population from 1929–2000, the longest run for a political party in human history. At the same time, the PRUD was unable to dominate elections as did the PRI, given examples such as the opposition party Renovating Action Party (PAR). Although isolated from the legislature by the PRUD, the PAR was still able to gain 43 percent of the vote in the 1950 elections.

President Osorio's successor, Colonel José María Lemus (1956–1960), only incurred more opposition with his attempt to balance socioeconomic reforms with pleasing the rich. The dissident movement in this case was the April and May Revolutionary Party (PRAM), which was made up of middle class and student groups as well as communists, representing the fact that the destruction of so many lives in the 1932 massacre of thousands of people failed to beat the people into submission as the military and elites had hoped. This movement quickly gained momentum by incorporating more people, eventually becoming the National Civic Orientation Front (FNOC). FNOC would factor into the coup that overthrew Lemus in 1960 along with military officers and the former president, Oscar Osorio.

THE "DEMOCRATIC" ERA, 1960–1972

The years 1960 through 1972 was considered to be the democratic era in Salvadoran political affairs due to the rise of a valid opposition movement under the banner of the Christian Democratic Party (PDC). This was similar to the rise of Christian Democrats across Latin America whereby combined elements of leftist intellectuals, elites, middle class, working class, and peasants worked together to form a political party with the ability to defeat the authoritarian elements both on the right and the left. In El Salvador, the right wing represented the traditional elites in the military and the so-called Fourteen Families, whereas the armed guerrilla factions that emerged in the 1970s represented the left. And although many former PDC proponents later joined these leftist guerrillas, the PDC of the 1960s sought to avoid both extremes while incorporating as wide of a spectrum as possible.

It is important to realize here that the Christian Democrats were not liberals in the same sense as their North American counterparts. Salvadoran liberals were closer in political ideology to North American conservatives, who sought to limit government control over social and economic sectors while promoting social justice to a degree and in particular relying on a firm policy of democratic elections versus authoritarianism. The Salvadoran liberal draws inspiration from western notions of development and political structure and as such promotes notions such as separation of powers firmly supported by effective checks and balances, separation of church and state, freedom of the press, and a reduced role for the military except in times of crisis.

Several elements spurred on this alternative movement. The Cuban Revolution provided an impetus due to its extreme nature. The fact that Castro had succeeded in overthrowing an established system right under the nose of the United States inspired many revolutionaries and frightened the more moderate and conservative elements in Latin America. As Castro, Khrushchev, Eisenhower, and later Kennedy battled over influence and control in the hemisphere, political actors on both sides felt more pressure to draw the line as left- and right-wing sympathizers risked being associated with the extremes. The Bay of Pigs debacle of 1961 and the Cuban Missile Crisis of 1962 only heightened tensions further, increasingly forcing Cuba out of favor within the Americas and as such delegitimizing elements associated with Castro's movement.

At the same time, the Kennedy and Johnson administrations attempted to stem the tide of Castroism. They approached this in two fashions. First, U.S. policy sought to contain and isolate Cuba through military, paramilitary, and diplomatic actions. Second, they sought to undermine the spread of leftwing revolutionary ideology and activity by sending aid to Latin American countries in order to support their economic growth. This occurred through projects such as the Alliance for Progress, which not all Latin American nations agreed to participate in, and which ultimately failed. However, El Salvador was one of the main countries where the Alliance was accepted as a solution to their ills. Kennedy first announced the Alliance in March 1961 and a hemisphere-wide agreement was reached on the plan in August 1961 in Punta del Este, Uruguay, just as debate over Castro's role in the Organization of the American States (OAS) was heating up due to his tilt toward the Soviet Union. The Alliance's goals were several, including a steady 2.5 percent increase in salaries nationwide, a shift away from dictatorship to democracy as a rule for governance, social and economic development, land reform, a drive to economic and social equality, education for all, and the reduction of inflation. As these goals recognized the common problems ailing Latin American societies, countries such as El Salvador realized how they could benefit and as such joined in with the U.S. program.

Another important impetus for the rise of the Christian democrats was the overthrow of the dictatorship of José María Lemus in 1960 and his eventual replacement by Julio Adalberto Rivera (1962–1967). Rivera jumped on the Alliance for Progress bandwagon and incurred great praise for his reforms from U.S. reporters, intellectuals, and officials who supported the program as well. However, within this atmosphere of reform, democracy in the different form emerged in the form of the Christian Democrats. As this viable opposition to the traditional elites rose popularly and quickly, it fell off the face of Salvadoran politics through fraud and violence perpetrated by those same conservative elements so closely aligned with the United States by 1972.

This was not uncommon throughout Latin America, as both established and budding democracies fell all around. Brazilian democracy crumbled with the U.S.-backed coup against Joao Goulart (1961–1964) in 1964, not to recover until 1985. Dominican flirtation with democracy disintegrated in the early to mid-1960s despite a U.S. invasion in 1965 to restore stability. Guatemala's 10 years of democracy had fallen apart in 1954 with the U.S. coup that overthrew Jacobo Arbenz (1951–1954), setting that country on a course of civil war that lasted until 1997. Perhaps the most well known of them all was the end of Chilean democracy in 1973, with the U.S.-backed overthrow of the democratically elected socialist president Salvador Allende (1970–1973). The year before General Augusto Pinochet (1973–1990) and his generals plunged Chile into a most undemocratic abyss of torture and disappearance from which it would not emerge for 17 years, El Salvador's dance with democracy ended in 1972 with the stolen elections that maintained power in the hands of the elites while further marginalizing the poor majority as well as most reformers.

1960: THE TURNING POINT

The year 1960 signifies an important break with past political processes in El Salvador and it begins with the measures taken by the Lemus dictatorship. José María Lemus began a roundup of dissidents throughout 1960 in response to civil unrest against his government that had begun the previous year. These roundups included official opponents as well as random individuals that suffered at the hands of his minions. By April, municipal and assembly elections threatened the ruling party's (PRUD) control as an umbrella opposition movement rose under FNOC. Elements of this movement had a long history of dissent against authoritarianism, as they had established their credentials in the 1944 general strike that pushed out the rule of General Martinez. The PAR coalition had cut their political teeth against Martinez as well, as did the PRAM, who drew its name from their two month long revolt against Martinez in 1944 and drew inspiration from the Cuban Revolution. While PRAM and PAR were different from one another, they teamed up behind PAR's candidates against the ruling party during the elections of 1960. However, PAR was only recognized in half of the 14 districts as a legitimate party and PRUD won all seats in the Legislative Assembly while losing only six mayoral elections to the PAR, which was something of a victory for the opposition.

Lemus soon instituted wider repression after the election results brought antigovernment protestors into the streets of San Salvador in September 1960. His state of siege rounded up dissidents in the same fashion as had occurred many times in Salvadoran history, with the usual unlawfulness leading to torture, beatings, and even death. As a result of Lemus's policies beginning the previous year, former president Oscar Osorio created his own version of the PRUD known as the Authentic PRUD, and quickly became a legitimate opposition figure to Lemus's rule. Then came the October 26 rebellion. It lasted five hours and was completely nonviolent, which went completely against the grain of Salvadoran, and indeed Latin American, history. The new junta established in San Salvador set about reforming the political system immediately by releasing political prisoners and dissolving the Supreme Court and the Legislative Assembly. Osorio's leadership of the coup incorporated dissidents from across the political spectrum, and the new junta, containing civilian intellectuals such as Fabio Castillo Figueroa, Ricardo Falla Caceres, and René Fortin Magaña, fomented an atmosphere of pluralism that led to the formation of nine legitimate political parties ready to participate in the elections of 1961, from which the Christian Democrats emerged as a powerful party. The party had originated among the wealthier elements of Salvadoran society inspired by post–World War II European Christian Democracy as early as 1958. Jose Napoleon Duarte was among its strongest members by 1960, and he would later become the PDC's candidate for president in 1972.

However, the new junta's experiment ended abruptly on January 25, 1961 under the force of an officers' rebellion that felt it necessary to thwart the power of what it considered to be a radical leftist government. It is important to note here that it had taken the United States two months to recognize the previous government out of fear it would turn Communist, and it immediately backed the January coup plotters for their efforts to stem that Communism despite the high level of violence perpetrated by the latter as opposed to the lack of violence on the part of the former. Still, the new junta, under the banner of the Civil-Military Directorate led by Colonels Julio Adalberto Rivera and Anibal Portillo, recognized that reform was necessary in order to prevent both right- and left-wing authoritarianism. Therefore, it eventually worked with the United States to acquire $25 million in aid for reforms in tune with the Alliance for Progress. Initial reforms were subtle but important, falling under the banner of the February *proclama* that drove two conservative civilians from the directorate. The *proclama* set the stage for such reforms as a labor law giving employees at least one day off per week, rent reductions, agrarian reform, and the nationalization of banks and other economic protectionist measures. These reforms soon morphed Rivera's Directorio into a political party known as the National Conciliation Party (PCN) by September 1961, just four months after Duarte was named secretary-general of the PDC.

The election campaign of late 1961 spelled a defeat for the three opposition groups that combined under the banner of the Union of Democratic Parties (UPD). The PDC participated within this group but due to an inability to unite ideologically, the PCN crushed the opposition, taking every seat in the assembly. Rivera eventually took over the presidency later that year after the April elections produced no opposition party candidates due to the internal bickering of the opposition parties.

Rivera's government lasted until 1967, during which time the face of Salvadoran politics changed while the power system favoring the smallest of elites within the military and the oligarchy continued largely unabated. Recognizing the popularity of democratic opposition groups, Rivera sought to reinvent himself as a man of the people through image and action. For example, he would dress in working class clothes in order to associate himself with the poor and he introduced reforms that sought to placate these classes while maintaining close ties to the elites who also depended on him in a sort of mutually reinforcing survival relationship. His reforms responded to the growing needs of the masses in the form of labor, land, and tax laws claiming to protect the poor. These laws were often ignored by elites or actually favored them, proving Rivera's programs ineffective even as he was touted as a beacon of hope by American planners of the Alliance for Progress. Taken as a whole, Rivera followed a similar plan to that of the military presidencies of the past three decades of quickly consolidating power through repression of opposition elements in order to pave the way toward implementing reforms. Just as had occurred in the past, the reforms of the 1960s did not ameliorate the misery of the poor majority and only served to increase the wealth of the tiny minority.

THE PROBLEM OF OPPOSITION PARTIES

The opposition parties, including the PAR, the PRAM, and the PDC, lacked a cohesive ideology with which to unite large amounts of dissidents under a solid banner enthusiastically opposed to the ruling party in 1961. This problem later dissipated, but in this early stage of opposition growth, there were several models of opposition across the hemisphere that had created themselves in the image of anti-dictatorship struggles successfully. Mexico's Institutional Revolutionary Party (PRI) and Venezuela's Democratic Action (AD) come to mind immediately, but this was El Salvador, with uniquely Salvadoran problems such as the heavy concentration on the power of the military and the consolidated elite.

The Christian Democrats provided an alternative to these reform movements that tilted more to the left of the spectrum, thus giving a voice to anti-Communists as well as anti-traditionalists, who often found themselves on opposite sides of the fence before Castroism arrived. Chile's Eduardo Frei (1964–1970) represented just such an example to follow and his defeat of Salvador Allende's socialist movement in 1964 only solidified the validity of Christian Democracy as an alternative both to socialism and reactionary militarism. The main unifying factor of the Christian Democrats was found in its name, as its affiliation with Catholicism legitimized it with a large portion of the population. However, this was only to the extent that it could prove itself not controlled by the church. Duarte and many others within the PDC leadership had formal Catholic university and clerical training as well, but their intellectual and business backgrounds also brought nonreligious issues such as property rights, democracy, land reform, and education to the front of their agendas.

In addition, the Christian Democrats could not be easily pegged down by either side of the political spectrum when it came to foreign policy perspectives. For example, the United States tended to support either Christian Democrats or right-wing elements across Latin America and indeed, the entire developing world, and yet, the Salvadoran Christian Democrats spoke as vociferously against U.S. interventions as they did against the Soviet Union's. Throughout the 1960s, they condemned U.S. actions against nations like Cuba and the Dominican Republic as acts of imperialism in the same manner in which they condemned the Soviets for similar actions in their own sphere of influence.

The PDC helped bring controversial issues into public debate during the 1960s. Land reform, education, private property rights, and democracy vs. dictatorship were all questioned during this period, as was the issue of the family's role in El Salvador. The PDC held up the family as the primary functioning unit within Salvadoran society just as the conservatives had done for years. A major Salvadoran problem of the twentieth century, as population numbers have skyrocketed, has been the preservation of two parent families. As family sizes have grown, work became sparser, and military repression targeted men primarily—many families consisted of a female breadwinner who also served as the lone parent throughout much of the year. Often times, men have spent long periods of time away in order to work on coffee or other agricultural plantations as well. Perhaps just as often, fathers have abandoned their families to fend for themselves. The PDC put forth a political platform in the 1960s to force fathers to support their families in an effort to incorporate more women (who gained the vote in 1945) into their party. This platform worked quickly and large sources of PDC support came eventually from the areas mostly staffed by women, such as the markets of San Salvador.

Thus, the PDC attempted to play a delicate balancing act within Salvadoran politics so as not to threaten anyone into reacting violently against their platform. This proved a difficult task within such an ever impoverishing country whose elite had depended on military force for protection and validation throughout its national history. Their land reform program sought to empower the landless peasantry while promoting an increase in agricultural exports. This ran the risk of alienating extremist elements on both sides that held suspicions about the PDC's leanings. In the end, the PDC's membership aligned closely with business interests and yet the threat they posed to the traditional elites was in its very existence as a genuine opposition movement. The PDC presented the only viable alternative to either extreme, whether on the left or the right, precisely because they could not be expected to hold to one side's prescribed view. They presented a multiplicity of programs and ideologies that claimed to seek to forge political change within a more democratic atmosphere that included action based on informed, pluralistic debate. While much of this was indeed pure political rhetoric, the PDC no doubt opened up Salvadoran politics to a more democratic way of operating. In the end, its ideals were rooted in concepts that sometimes contradicted modern notions of democracy. Their roots in Catholicism, as well as their notions about women returning to the home and abandoning the workplace, are examples of their inability to truly court the masses. This platform was only to last until the 1972 elections when the traditionalists were able to thwart this rising tide of democratic culture and replace it with military rule anew.

Nevertheless, the PDC gained considerable ground throughout the 1960s. Duarte was elected mayor of the capital in 1964 and served three consecutive terms until 1970 when he began preparing for a presidential bid for the 1972 elections. By 1968, the PDC had nearly 40 percent control over the legislative assembly and even began passing its own party's laws. This represented an ever growing danger to the power of the PCN, who had won the presidency of 1967 with Colonel Fidel Sanchez Hernandez (1967–1972). Sanchez ordered the National Guard to crack down on political and labor dissent. The Guard's new head was Colonel Jose Alberto Medrano, an officer who acquired funds to increase the activities of ORDEN, which was used both for public service and to spy on, intimidate, and liquidate the opposition, namely in the countryside. It was during this period that U.S. military assistance expanded, with the mindset that any dissent against the government must be illegitimate. The result was support for repressive regime after repressive regime in El Salvador, lasting until 1992.

THE SOCCER WAR, 1969

In the midst of the PNC's struggle to preserve power and the PDC's struggle to acquire it, a war broke out between Honduras and El Salvador in 1969. Problems had been mounting for a while before the outbreak of war, which was largely due to trade within the Central American Common Market (CACM) and the large number of Salvadorans working in Honduras, with migrant waves dating back to the early 1900s. The Honduran government began expelling Salvadorans in 1969 in response to the landed elite's concerns over their ability to preserve their own lands amid the rising needs of Honduran peasants for their own lands, and on several occasions fights broke out at soccer matches between Salvadorans and Hondurans. The Salvadoran military invaded Honduras and quickly claimed victory, but in reality the war came to a stalemate after just over five days. The opposition within El Salvador was quickly quelled as a result of the rising nationalism created by the war, and the PCN increased its power as a result.

While the surface level results of the war spelled political victory for the PCN, there were residual effects of the Soccer War of 1969 that would build up for the next two decades. A large majority of the thousands of refugees that fled the violence in Honduras escaped just across the border to the northern Salvadoran provinces of Cabañas, Chalatenango, and Morazán, the very provinces most pervaded by leftist guerrillas during the civil war of the 1980s. These refugees returned to an even poorer El Salvador than they had left. The war also helped motivate radicalized leftists from the (Partido Comunista Salvadoreno (PCS) and even disillusioned members of the PDC to take up arms in the 1970s. The first guerrilla faction, the Popular Forces of Liberation—Farabundo Martí (FPL) was formed by former PCS activist Salvador Cayetano Carpio in 1970, and the People's Revolutionary Army (ERP) was formed in 1971. The official political repression against people associated with these forces would only increase in the 1970s as a result.

However, even as politics continued down the road toward eventual chaos and violence, El Salvador's economy improved markedly. Economic planners shifted priorities away from a strictly coffee-based (90%) export market to increase support for cotton and sugar as well as a newly established manufacturing industry. Of course, the Central American Common Market (CACM) ended after the Soccer War, but until then, El Salvador had taken full advantage of the common market to expand economically. The increasing population size stemmed the benefits of this economic growth, however, which in turn caused more emigration to other countries such as Honduras, which created a factor for war between the two countries in 1969, which then, ironically, caused the end of the common market.

THE END OF THE "DEMOCRATIC" ERA, 1970–1972

Even as the PCN had attempted to placate the right and the poor majority in the 1960s, it proved transparently incapable of doing so for either side by 1971.

The popularity of the war of 1969 could not carry the party forever, and by 1971 and 1972, the opposition parties of the right as well as moderates within the PDC stood a real chance of challenging the PCN in the 1972 elections. The PDC was able to unite competing factions in the center and left under one umbrella and the PNC lost support from large numbers of rightists. In particular, the conservatives became enraged at President Sanchez's remarks in September 1970 emphasizing the need for social justice programs in El Salvador that might improve the lot of the majority poor. Salvadoran elites accused Sanchez of playing the Communist game and vehemently opposed him from that point on. Soon negative attention came to the National University, with the kidnapping and murder of one of the nation's most prominent elite sons, Ernesto Regalado Dueñas in February 1971. Conservatives blamed the murder on leftists from the university and found in this another excuse for promoting widespread fear against the so-called rise of Communism in El Salvador. The university was later targeted by death squads in the 1970s and 1980s due to allegations of Communist subversion on the part of professors and students.

For the elections of 1972, the PDC united with the Nationalist Democratic Union (UDN) and the National Revolutionary Movement (MNR) to form the National Opposing Union (UNO). As the PDC represented the largest faction with the largest following, it naturally followed that the PDC's platform would form the centerpiece of UNO's platform. The PCN put forth President Sanchez's secretary, Colonel Arturo Armando Molina, but there were two alternative right-wing opposition candidates that represented elite and military interests, from the Salvadoran Popular Party (PPS) and the United Independent Democratic Front (FUDI). While the PPS stood little chance, the candidate of the FUDI, General Jose Alberto Medrano, was soon arrested for the murder of a policeman who happened to be assigned to the Regalado kidnapping/murder investigation, raising the question of Medrano's possible role in the crime. On election day, February 20, the country seemed to be going Duarte's way after it was announced that he had won San Salvador by a ratio of 2:1 over Molina. However, as soon as announcements were coming in about UNO's rising poll numbers, the government called a halt to these announcements, and by morning, announced a victory over UNO, even though records from the voting departments showed a defeat for Molina in favor of Duarte. When the election results came to a vote on the floor of the Legislative Assembly at an earlier date than was scheduled, the UNO party delegates were unprepared and the vote went off without UNO's participation. As a result, the PCN delegates voted in Molina under a tremendous cloud of corruption.

Then came the coup attempt of March 25 by Colonel Benjamin Mejia. Mejia's men captured the president and his daughter and quickly declared victory, albeit without reason because although he commanded the Salvadoran army, the National Guard, the Air Force, the National Police, and the Treasury Police were still available to put down the revolt. Duarte's eventual support of the revolt raised questions as to his involvement from the beginning. Whatever the case, the revolt was quickly suppressed and Duarte eventually found refuge in Venezuela, effectively ending the experiment with democracy that the Christian Democrats had built. El Salvador would have to go through 20 more years of conflict before democracy would take hold, and would lose between 70,000 and 80,000 lives through violence in the process.

7

Revolution, 1972–1992

The road to the civil war in El Salvador is a chronology of desperation. It explains the problems of the present and the past, and it has given outsiders a manual on both how not to and how to solve internal disputes. For the path to conflict shows us how horrific the consequences can be when human beings refuse to listen to others, while the resolution to the war shows us what is possible when they do finally set their weapons down and hear each other out. The case of El Salvador demonstrates this all too painfully. What follows is the story of the path and progression of one of the most devastating Latin American civil wars of the past century.

The Molina presidency that followed the 1972 election debacle was not the first blow in the road to war. It was the election itself. And once Arturo Molina took control he further exacerbated the tensions by setting in motion a wave of anti-Communist nationalism that spun out of control to the point that it dominated federal policy for the next two decades. Aside from the guerrillas that would soon gain control of much of the countryside, the government began to target university students, who served as a perfect scapegoat for their own problems. As Molina's presidency suffered from questions of his legitimacy due to the attempted coup, electoral corruption, and the oligarchy's fear of reforms that would threaten their high degree of wealth, he hoped his actions against students would solidify his image as a strong leader. The military was ordered to occupy three campuses of the University of El Salvador from 1972 to 1973, fully instilling fear into the minds of left-leaning professors and students alike, as well as instigating many among them to resist with more force (in fact, many felt forced into joining the guerrillas as a result of this occupation). These actions pleased the ultraconservative oligarchy whose fears only became more realizable as a result, for the military only provided yet another reason for nonviolent resisters to take up arms.

Molina promulgated the idea that the students on university campuses associated with the University of El Salvador were subverting the system with communist agitation. He responded to this concern by ending the university's independence from government interference, placing a government official in charge of the college, and ordering the military to occupy the campuses. In response to this and other measures carried out under the Molina regime, university students began protesting in Santa Ana and San Salvador until the government carried out yet another massacre, this time in San Salvador. This standard response by the military led to another 37 deaths in the streets of the capital. Other massacres took place amid the increase in repression, such as the killing of at least six peasants at La Cayetana in November of 1974.

It must be remembered that violence has been an integral part of El Salvador's history from the beginning of the republic on all sides of the political battlefield. Just as *La Matanza* was the response on the part of the Salvadoran generals to a real uprising that terrorized people, albeit on a scale much smaller than was portrayed by the Martinez government, so too was the repression under Molina a response to an ever-increasing wave of violence perpetrated by armed factions opposed to the government. The 1970s was the era in which the guerrillas that posed such a formidable obstacle to the government in the 1980s began to congeal as cohesive units with widespread support from the poor, working class, and intellectuals.

The government and its right-wing supporters in particular responded to the left-wing threats with increasingly creative means by the mid-1970s. In 1975, the Anti-Communist Wars of Liberation Armed Forces (FALANGE) emerged as an example of this. Their mission was to uproot all leftist opposition and its supporters through force, and they were eventually joined by many other factions with the same goal, increasing in numbers exponentially in tandem with the inevitable increase in guerrillas and their supporters. ORDEN was another group, already established, with this same purpose. The members of these organizations tended to be former or current armed forces officers who operated with impunity due to their intimate connections to the oligarchy and the military within which and for whom they functioned.

The elections of 1976 proved to be another difficult year in Salvadoran politics, namely because the opposition National Opposing Union (UNO) party abstained due to allegations of fraud in the past two elections in 1972 and 1974. However, Molina did attempt to placate concerns of the poor majority by enacting a land reform program in San Miguel and Usulutan in which 12,000 families would receive 61,000 hectares of land. This was made possible under a 1975 law that allowed the government to redistribute fallow land to those without land. The administration of this program fell under the new organization, the Salvadoran Institute of Agrarian Transformation (ISTA). The term "reform" was considered taboo due to its leftist connotations, and thus the term "transformation" was used in its place. The oligarchy immediately signaled their disgust, and Molina received threats of an overthrow if he proceeded with the program. As a result, the project was abandoned and the status quo remained.

Not surprisingly, the economic interests that had dominated El Salvador for a century by the 1970s would only continue apace as long as it was possible. Industrial growth, linked to foreign investment and the maintenance of the coffee-growing elite that supported it, led to the further dichotomization of the country's classes in geographical terms. Although coffee growing obviously took place outside of the cities, the investment of capital resulting from the coffee industry was inherently concentrated in the cities, leading to increased poverty in the countryside, and thus augmenting the reasons why peasants took up arms in support of the guerrillas.

The elections of 1977 signified yet another crucial year for the future of El Salvador. UNO attempted to reenter the political arena by placing its candidate Ernesto Claramont for president. Election day was full of fraudulent actions on the party of the dominant National Conciliation Party (PCN) party, which wreaked havoc across the country with violence, intimidation, and ballot stuffing in order to win the election. In response to this fraud, Claramont and his followers staged a demonstration in San Salvador's Plaza Libertad that eventually grew to 50,000, which lasted until February 28 when the National Police attacked the protesters, killing close to 50, and driving Claramont into exile.

The aftermath of the massacre at Plaza Libertad and the election of the PCN's candidate Carlos Humberto Romero (1977–1979) only further solidified the road to civil war. The United States facilitated this path even as it claimed to prevent it through its policies enacted under the new president, Jimmy Carter (1977–1981). Carter's policy of using human rights as a standard for U.S. foreign relations was deemed too light on Communism for right-wing elements in the United States and El Salvador and Carter sometimes gave in to that side by sending military aid and advisors to the Salvadoran military, which used death squads to carry out the kinds of human rights abuses generally deplored by the Carter administration. Romero soon justified a massive increase in repression against so-called revolutionary or subversive elements in response to a real rise in the number of kidnappings and murders of the military and the upper classes on the part of guerrillas. However, the majority of those targeted were unarmed noncombatants, and this only further infuriated the peasantry and even the church, which became an activist arm of the opposition to the government. Romero operated under a very official-sounding law known as The Law for the Defense and Guarantee of the Public Order, which gave the state the right to arrest anyone it suspected of being a subversive.

THE RISE OF THE RESISTANCE

The Salvadoran civil war's roots trace far back in time, as we have observed, but in 1970, the first of the five revolutionary organizations that eventually formed the umbrella group of the FMLN (Farabundo Martí Liberation Front) began. This guerrilla movement would eventually challenge the military apparatus so much that repression increased exponentially against the civilian population. By 1981, violence had reached the point where official military massacres of whole villages were commonplace, such as the case of El Mozote in December of that year, when 900 civilians were killed by the elite Atlacatl Battalion. An equally little publicized phenomenon also became known that year: the military's use of the guillotine to execute political dissidents. The death squads were also known for using meat slaughterhouse saws to decapitate dissidents as an example to all those who would dare oppose them, even if those means were nonviolent.

At the same time, many nonviolent resistance groups that had formed under the tutelage of activist-minded priests beginning in the 1960s, increased their efforts at democratic change only to find themselves repressed even more so by the death squads. Eventually, by the end of the decade, many of these activists were forced to join the guerrillas in armed struggle against the government. The first group was the FPL (Popular Liberation Front), which was created from the remnants of the outlawed Salvadoran Communist Party (PCS or Partido Comunista Salvadoreno) that was crushed with such ferocity by the military government in *La Matanza* of 1932. The secretary general of the PCS, Cayetano Carpio decided to help form the FPL in 1970 when it was deemed necessary to take up arms and spread word of the revolution once again. Carpio's reasoning as explained in a 1980 interview relied on the logic that the Salvadoran people had suffered enough marginalization and that they were prepared to rise in revolt with the proper support from fellow Salvadorans that were prepared to fight. The fact that the PCS's membership had been severely repressed over the course of the past four decades was present in their minds upon their embarkation of this new plan, and they went ahead anyway.

By 1972, an additional revolutionary group emerged named the ERP (People's Revolutionary Army) as yet another product of the old PCS and contained both younger generation radical revolutionaries from the Young Communists as well as members of the clergy and the elites. In fact, several members were dedicated Catholic and Protestant activists. The ERP followed revolutionary icon Che Guevara's *foco* theory of revolution that relied on the concept of smaller, focused guerrilla communities that spread revolution through concentrated efforts within civilian enclaves. It also followed the rationale that large armies were unnecessary to begin a revolution, for the *focos* themselves would expand the struggle into a larger movement eventually through their own merits. They also created the RN (National Resistance or Resistencia Nacional) movement as well as the FAPU (United Popular Action Front) to organize within different communities. The ERP eventually suffered from internal divisions that led to the militant wing of the group to condemn one of their own who was El Salvador's most beloved modern poet, Roque Dalton, to death in 1975.

Soon, other resistance-oriented groups formed, such as the FARN (Armed Forces of National Resistance), the UDN (the political front organization of the PCS), and others both armed and unarmed. The PCS, however, became even more dedicated to the expansion of armed struggle after the massacre at La Plaza Libertad. That year signaled the beginning of a downward spiral of violence that soon engulfed most of the Salvadoran countryside, mostly carried out by the government.

ARTISTS AMID ANARCHY

The story of Roque Dalton (1935–1975) tells us the story of El Salvador. Dalton would become one of the most famous Salvadoran poets, and yet he would die not at the hands of those he opposed, but at the hands of those he helped. At the University of El Salvador he was part of the University Literary Circle in 1956, and witnessed repression at the hands of the military, which destroyed the building in which it was housed. He published his first book, *Mine with the Birds* in 1958. He visited Russia and became a Communist soon after, and was incarcerated in 1959 and 1960 on the charges of inciting insurrection in El Salvador. He was slated for execution in 1960 when the Lemus dictatorship was overthrown and he was let out. He then went to Mexico the following year where he wrote *The Injured Party's Turn* (1962) and *The Window in My Face* (1961).

He was first and foremost a revolutionary, and therefore he headed for Cuba in 1961 and got to know other revolutionary writers and underwent guerrilla training. He returned to El Salvador in 1965 and was soon arrested and received the death sentence again. An earthquake hit soon afterward and he escaped and made his way to Cuba and then to Prague where he worked as a writer for *The International Review: Problems of Peace and Socialism.* His time in

Prague resulted in *Tavern and Other Places* in 1969. He returned to Cuba where he planned to join the guerrillas in Guatemala known as the Guerrilla Army of the Poor (EGP) but this never panned out and he stayed in Cuba for years with the famous Casa de las Americas publishing more books and writing for *Prensa Latina*.

Before reaching 40 of years of age, he would produce 18 books. However, his life was cut short by his fellow revolutionaries who executed him on suspicion of being a Central Intelligence Agency (CIA) spy. He had joined the Popular Revolutionary Army (ERP) in 1973 and by 1975 was clearly at odds with the leadership. Dalton's ideology followed the line of reasoning that the armed wing of the revolution must be one with unarmed organizations working in tandem to overthrow the government. The leadership of the ERP saw this as treachery and had him shot. His last book, *Clandestine Poems* (1975), was published just before his death. There were other Salvadoran authors but none as well known as Dalton took up arms to back up his writing, and for that, he revered even more so than the rest.

Although not a traditional revolutionary himself, Fernando Llort (1949–) is another artist greatly affected by the conflict in the 1970s. He is considered El Salvador's greatest painter and he began the folk art genre of the town of La Palma in the mountains of Chalatenango north of San Salvador. He created the Center for Integral Development and the Seed of God, which are places for artists to work and learn. His San Salvador gallery, God's Tree, is internationally known and his paintings are in the Metropolitan Cathedral in San Salvador. He is known for his vivid colorful paintings that resemble Picasso while bringing his own unique Salvadoran style to the work. He drew his inspiration from several trips abroad as a student of art in France, Belgium, and the United States. He noted how this time in strange lands called on his expressive talents to reveal his own Salvadoran identity. Upon return to El Salvador, Llort stayed in La Palma for six years (1973–1979) where he fine-tuned his painting style until he felt forced to flee the area due to the growing war atmosphere, and he went to San Salvador, where he was born. His style, which includes acrylics, oil, and other materials, has been described by many as child-like yet incredibly insightful and deep in meaning and feeling.

ESCALATION

Despite the presence of higher thinkers such as Dalton and Llort, the country was headed down an irreversible road to war. In 1977, the armed forces assassinated the popular priest-activist Rotulio Grande, who was the close friend of the archbishop of San Salvador and also future martyr, Oscar Romero. Father Grande's murder in particular signified the absolute lack of limits on the armed forces of El Salvador, and it sent shockwaves throughout the church. It was not just that a priest had been killed, but it shed light on the fact that many other priests, nuns, and lay church organizers had been killed defending their flocks, which had been dying in high numbers as well throughout El Salvador. Grande, like many of his fellow left-leaning church workers, had taken up the mantle of Liberation Theology, a philosophy that a minority within the Latin American Catholic Church had ascribed to ever since the 1960s that aimed to represent the interests of the poor majority of the population. Grande had firsthand knowledge of the inequalities and violence that had been consistently perpetrated by the Salvadoran elite and military governments down the years and felt it necessary to stand next to and in front of his parishioners. This was an attitude that those in power could not abide, and he paid for this with his life. The idea was to send a message to all others who would oppose the government, just as this was the message of all the past political assassinations and mass murders.

By 1979, this repression had fully entrenched the cycle of violence, making it inevitable that thousands of resistance activists would take up arms against the government to survive. However, in 1979, many civilians in resistance still remained nonviolent and mobilized thousands to pressure the government to stop the repression, only to risk arrest, torture, and slaughter at their hands. The growth in the number of armed bands grew quickly thereafter, and by 1979, they had joined to form the FAL (Armed Forces of Liberation). Guerrillas both old and new responded with equal violence against the government armed forces, using kidnappings and executions as favored tactics. The process of settling political problems by way of the gun on both sides must be seen, however, in the context of El Salvador's long and violent past, in which conquistadors, colonizers, Indians, slaves, independence leaders, nationalists, military leaders, and resistance fighters have utilized violence to affect change.

By the 1970s, the government was used to responding to the growth of alternative movements by creating instruments of mass repression. The two prominent organizations it formed in this decade were ORDEN and the UCS (Salvadoran Communal Union). ORDEN often worked as a death squad unit that served as the precursor to La Mano Blanca, later headed by Colonel Roberto D'Aubuisson, the founder of the currently dominant political party, Nationalist Republican Alliance (ARENA). ORDEN was accompanied by the UCS that was created with the help of the AIFLD (American Institute for Free Labor Development). The UCS attempted to influence poor peasants to join in with the government's agrarian reform program, but was devastated by government death squads that massacred many associated peasants. A faction of the UCS eventually joined up with the FAPU in 1978, feeling they were left with little other options for reform.

The year 1979 accelerated El Salvador's race to all-out civil war with a series of crucial events. First, the Romero government's arrest of revolutionaries led to a protest of several hundred people in San Salvador that year that ended in government-sponsored bloodshed in May. The next two events occurred in neighboring Nicaragua later that summer. The end of the Somoza dictatorship dynasty that had lasted from 1936 to 1979 was precipitated by one of the most successful Latin American revolutions of the twentieth century. The Sandinistas overthrew the last Somoza, Anastasio "Tachito" Somoza Debayle in a popular revolt that culminated on July 17, 1979. Soon afterward, many officers of the hated National Guard fled north through Honduras and El Salvador, sending the message to Salvadoran officers and elites that if they were not careful, they could be next in losing everything as well. Thus, the counter-revolutionary resolve of the Salvadoran elite and military sectors strengthened as a result of the Sandinista victory in Nicaragua.

The Romero government was on its last leg by this time, and a group of coup plotters led by civilians as well as military men met little resistance in carrying out their mission on October 15, 1979. In spite of the lack of popularity of the coup, the military faction under Colonel Jaime Abdul Gutierrez soon ruled the day, which discouraged the civilian wing of the revolt. The idea was to eliminate the growing insurgency above implementing the needed social and economic reforms the population had been calling for that had initially allowed for support for the insurgencies to begin with. At the same time, the elites were soon discouraged by the reform portion of the new junta's agenda.

The U.S. presidency of Jimmy Carter soon took on a two track policy toward El Salvador in light of the new events. The first aspect of this included a military support program of U.S. weapons and advisors and the second included support for democratic goals. Whether or not the U.S. government cared to know the extent of the repression carried out by the junta and its right wing followers is in question. What is certain is that the policy of human rights propagated by the Carter administration did not include an efficient verification standard in which U.S. officials sought to oversee the use of U.S. assistance to the Salvadoran military as it claimed to be hunting down subversives, when in actuality the vast majority of its victims were unarmed civilians. This has been established by innumerable sources, including the 1992 United Nations report released in 1992. In any case, by December of 1979, the junta fell apart.

January 1980 signaled an important shift in the direction of the country, albeit briefly, as attempts were made to restore the power of the junta under joint civilian-military control that included the Christian Democratic Party (PDC). On January 5, three civilians left the junta and were replaced by two more. By March, former presidential candidate Jose Napoleon Duarte joined the junta in a further effort to balance power in the face of the rising influence of the military. The military voices were gaining considerable ground during this period due to the increase in left-wing violence as well, which made it difficult for voices from the Christian Democrats to be heard. Meanwhile, the outgoing U.S. Ambassador Frank Devine was replaced by Robert White, who would last a year and still play an important part in the future of U.S.-Salvadoran relations. White in fact later went on to accuse Colonel Roberto D'Aubuisson of masterminding the assassination of Archbishop Romero and he become a critic of the Reagan administration's policies along with other State Department officials, most well known among them Wayne Smith, the former U.S. interest section chief in Cuba from 1979–1982. White and the Carter administration mostly continued the same two-track policy, which flew in the face of what was necessary for most Salvadorans. The military was able to use the assistance from the United States to kill upward of 10,000 mostly civilians that year.

Additionally, in January 1980, most members of revolutionary groups decided to put aside their differences and join the umbrella organization of the CRM (Revolutionary Coordination of the Masses) that uniformly sought an armed resolution to the crises of the country. That same month, a demonstration of 200,000 memorializing *La Matanza* of 1932 was put down by armed government units. The dead numbered at 49, with hundreds more injured. By March, the popular Archbishop Romero had been assassinated by the death squads, and these two events only solidified the resistance. By October, with tens of thousands of Salvadorans working both in unarmed and armed opposition to the governing junta that had taken power in 1979, the formidable guerrilla organization of the FMLN was formed from the four dominant guerrilla groups of the FPL, RN, ERP, and the CRTC (Central American Revolutionary Workers Party).

There were two incidents in particular that occurred in 1980 that awoke the consciousness of Americans and Salvadorans alike. The first was the assassination of the Archbishop of San Salvador, Oscar Arnulfo Romero (1917–1980), a conservative priest turned peace advocate and liberation theologian. Father Romero had a history of catering to the interests of the military and the oligarchy until the 1977 assassination by the military death squads of his friend Father Rutilio Grande. Father Grande's only crime was to take the side of the unarmed, poor Salvadorans experiencing repression from the military.

The archbishop had been chosen as a successor to Luis Chavez y Gonzalez precisely for his loyalties to the elites and was therefore targeted by those elites when he turned on them by speaking out both during his sermons and on his weekly radio program. He was an orator of the highest quality, which served him well both as a priest and as a leader of nonviolent opposition to the military government. He drew inspiration from Mahatma Gandhi and Martin Luther King and has served as an inspiration to people on many levels. His liberation theological leanings were symbolically important due to his high stature within the church because liberation theology was largely practiced by low-level priests who were often the target of government repression.

Thus, Father Romero's stance placed him both at risk and in a position of authority within this mostly fringe movement within Latin America that called on serving the poor first. He also inspired Salvadorans in general for his willingness to stand up to the armed forces of El Salvador unapologetically. He was unabashedly against the military's use of force in the civil war because he witnessed firsthand the result, which was the widespread devastation of poor communities across the country. Father Romero even inspired activists outside of El Salvador, both within Latin America and the United States. U.S. organizations opposed to the use of U.S. military assistance to the death squads in Central America drew on Romero's teachings for their own work. One example of this was the activism of U.S. Catholic Maryknoll priest and founder of School of the Americas Watch (SOAW) Father Roy Bourgeois, who with several others once snuck into the section of Fort Benning's military base where Salvadoran military officers were training at the U.S. Army School of the Americas (SOA) and played Father Romero's most famous speech (from March 23, 1980, the day before he was assassinated) in stereo from atop a tree, just before being attacked by Salvadoran soldiers:

> Brothers, you came from our own people. You are killing your own brothers. Any human order to kill must be subordinated to the law of God, which says, 'Thou shalt not kill'. No soldier is obliged to obey an order contrary to the law of God. No one has to obey an immoral law. It is high time you obeyed your consciences rather than sinful orders. The church cannot remain silent before such an abomination. . . . In the name of God, in the name of this suffering people whose cry rises to heaven more loudly each day, I implore you, I beg you, I order you: stop the repression![1]

The legacy of Father Romero lives on in the church as well, for he has been under review by the Vatican for beatification for 11 years. It was later discovered that Major Roberto D'Aubuisson, a graduate of the School of the Americas, had ordered the archbishop's assassination. Father Romero's funeral services were also interrupted by government violence that ended in the deaths of up to 50 mourners.

Unfortunately, Grande and Romero were only a small fraction of the victims belonging to advocates of nonviolence from the church in El Salvador in those years. In fact, there were many more. The most famous of these was certainly that of Father Romero himself due to the attention he had drawn before his death and due to his example that lasted for decades afterward.

The second most well-known incident occurred in November of 1980. Four church women helping unarmed war refugees in El Salvador were raped and murdered by five members of the security forces, three of which were School of the Americas graduates themselves. Maura Clarke, Ita Ford, Dorothy Kazel, and Jean Donovan had served the people selflessly even as most other volunteers had begun leaving the war-ravaged country. They represented the same threat to power represented by Fathers Grande and Romero because they sought to protect those being persecuted by the military-oligarchy alliance. Several books and many articles have been written about the lives and legacies of Romero and the church women, but less has been written on Father Grande, mainly because of the later more high-profile cases. The case of the four church women actually caused the Carter administration to temporarily suspend military aid to El Salvador, only to have it restored just before the Reagan administration took over the following year amid a surge of FMLN attacks against the government.

ENTER REAGAN, 1981–1989

The war had experienced ups and downs in 1980, with the guerrillas' supporters surging in the face of increasing repression. The Carter administration had supplied military hardware and intelligence to the Salvadoran military in the hopes of shaping the outcome in favor of peace and stability and found that the violence only increased as a result. The resulting cut off of aid only highlighted the tenuous nature of the military forces when compared to the widespread support enjoyed by the guerrillas, who also possessed an enormous willingness to fight and die for their cause. The restoration of military aid at the end of the Carter administration paled by comparison to the aid increase under Presidents Ronald Reagan (1981–1989) and George H. W. Bush (1989–1993). While Carter had supplied less than $6 million in military aid in 1980, Reagan and Bush provided over $4 billion in military aid for a decade to finance the war.

The year 1981 proved to be nearly as bloody as the previous year. It began with the inauguration of Ronald Reagan to the pleasure of the ranks of the Salvadoran military and oligarchy and to the displeasure of those supporting the guerrillas, and ended with the massacre at El Mozote that killed over 900 unarmed civilians. The incident at El Mozote took place in December as part of the army's general pattern of rolling through areas with any connections to the guerrillas. In the case of El Mozote and the surrounding villages, there was little guerrilla support but their location was close to the guerrilla stronghold at Perquín, just north of the area. The battalion responsible for the massacre was the Atlacatl Battalion, which was supported and trained by the U.S. military. In fact, 10 of the 12 officers in charge were graduates of the School of the Americas, including the commander, Lt. Col. Domingo Monterrosa.

Monterrosa's intelligence claimed that the villages surrounding El Mozote were supporting subversives, but this was merely a justification to attack the town. The army moved in full force, occupying the villages, and systematically murdering the men, women, and children by the hundreds over the course of several days. There were some survivors in the small hamlets nearby El Mozote, but in the case of El Mozote itself, there was only one, Rufina Amaya, who lived through the elimination of her entire family and village. She saved herself through hiding in the bushes when the opportunity presented itself, and lived to tell her story to the world. Shortly after the massacre, several American reporters got wind of the events and went to El Mozote to document the story. Reporters Raymond Bonner and Alma Guillermoprieto interviewed survivors and took pictures, reporting their findings in January 1982 in *The New York Times* and *The Washington Post.* The massacre stories drew criticism against the Reagan administration to which it responded that the evidence was not credible, essentially dismissing Bonner and Guillermoprieto's findings.

Once the United Nation's (UN) Truth Commission on the civil war in El Salvador was released at the end of the war, there was no question that in fact a U.S.-trained battalion of Salvadoran soldiers had massacred between 700 and 900 unarmed civilians in and around El Mozote in December of 1981. It was the worst single massacre of the war, but there would be others that reached the range of hundreds as well. For example, the Ramon Belloso Battalion, also trained and equipped by the U.S. government, killed untold hundreds of civilians deemed supporters of the FMLN in Chalatenango in May 1982. Of course, the FMLN was also engaged in attacks on the military itself and sometimes on civilians as well, but almost always avoided targeting civilians and usually avoided collateral damage as well.

During this period, the United States became more and more involved in Central America as a whole, with its main concern the triumph of the Sandinistas in Nicaragua in July 1979. The U.S. policy in El Salvador flowed from this, for they feared, as did many Salvadorans, a repeat of Nicaragua in El Salvador. The Sandinistas also participated in this process by supporting initiatives toward peace that were sponsored by the FMLN, to which the Reagan administration responded with harsh rebuffs. Instead, Reagan sought to isolate the Sandinistas even further through several methods. The first was to support the Contras, a group of mostly former National Guardsmen from the Somoza dictatorship that had fled north to Honduras in an effort to oppose the Sandinista government and supposedly to halt the flow of weapons between Nicaragua and El Salvador, for which there was scant evidence to begin with.

The Contras would later factor into the infamous Iran/Contra scandal in which the Reagan administration was caught selling weapons to Iranian terrorists for the purposes of using the profits to illegally fund the Contras. Another tactic Reagan used was to attempt to build regional alliances composing Costa Rica, Guatemala, Honduras, and El Salvador in order to push Nicaragua into backing down. The peace efforts continued throughout the 1980s, with the United States consistently siding with the military of El Salvador and the Contras.

In 1982, the United States worked to support elections in El Salvador that appeared free and fair. However, the end result was the perpetuation of the century-old allegiance between the military and the oligarchy, for they held the fundamental power in the country. At the same time, the United States represented a new power player in El Salvador and the elections were an example of this. Several authors have referred to the elections of 1982 as demonstration elections due to the fact that the elections were the brainchild of the Reagan administration that needed to legitimize the government it was supporting with such high levels of military hardware. By 1982, upward of 30,000 were dead and there were already 600,000 refugees in El Salvador. The U.S. government had to prove to its constituents that their tax dollars were going toward democratic goals, not merely to death squads as many believed. And they had some reason to believe this way judging from the headlines, which were still few and far between with the exception of articles about significant events such as the killings of Romero, the church women, and El Mozote, for example. However, the vast majority of those killed by the military received no attention at all from the U.S. press.

The elections introduced a new political party, ARENA, which has been in power since 1994. ARENA was founded with the leadership of Roberto D'Aubuisson in May 1981 along with many others of the Salvadoran right-wing, and they received their support from right-wing elements in the United States and were inspired in part by neo-Nazism. Their symbol and mantra were borrowed directly from the Dominican dictator, Rafael Leonidas Trujillo, who ruled over the small island nation for 30 years, killing tens of thousands of Dominicans and Haitians, also with the support of the United States government. However, the CIA and the Reagan administration deemed it more feasible to support the moderates such as the Christian Democrats as opposed to D'Aubuisson's followers in ARENA. The FMLN did not support the elections because it was excluded from the proceedings, and therefore it carried out several attacks on the government forces and intimidated people away from voting. The elections resulted in a strange turn of events, for even though the Christian Democrats led by Duarte won 40 percent of the votes, the right-wing parties under ARENA bound together to create a majority in the Legislative

Assembly. Alvaro Magaña of the Christian Democrats was named president and lasted until 1984.

D'Aubuisson quickly amassed power to himself, first becoming the president of the Legislative Assembly, then getting another death squad leader, Hector Antonio Regalado, named head of the Assembly's security. The U.S. response was not to admonish but to support these actions. The U.S. ambassador to El Salvador, Deane Hinton, in fact erased previous reports he had made of D'Aubuisson's antidemocratic aspirations and death squad activities, and U.S. Secretary of State General Alexander Haig pushed the Salvadoran government to overhaul its image in order to attempt to *appear* to be protecting human rights and promoting democratic ideals.

The Reagan administration learned to work with and persuade the government in El Salvador in a give and take manner as can be seen from the above descriptions. In this way, they were also able to provide the military with what it wanted while also controlling the conduct of the war to a degree. A 1983 report concluded that the U.S. officers in El Salvador had a large hand in the day-to-day activities of the military, not just in the area of training but also in the actual ground and air tactics used to prosecute the war itself.

The Battle of Moscarrón

Going by the pseudonym of Comandante "Ruiz," former ERP guerrilla commander Ruddy Amaya explained the details and significance of the most important strategic victory achieved by the FMLN during the war. The battle took place at Moscarrón, Morazán in June 1982. Until that point, the guerrillas had received little outside assistance and instead had relied on small arms and their wits more than anything else. The guerillas had realized several important things over that summer that led them to act in a decisive way. First, the March election campaigns portrayed the guerrillas as ineffective. Second, the Falkland Islands conflict between Argentina and Great Britain taking place between March and June is believed by the guerrillas to have diverted U.S. attention away from El Salvador briefly. Therefore, seizing the opportunity, the ERP mobilized 1,000 of its members into northern Morazán, where the Salvadoran military had outposts in every town. Phase I of the operation ended when the ERP took over the town of Perquín after intense fighting, which they held until the end of the war as a result. In Phase II, the ERP formed a "V" formation to envelope three military companies in three days of combat. In the end, the guerrillas claimed to have captured or killed over 300 soldiers. This precipitated the mobilization of 2,000 U.S.-backed Honduran troops to the border with El Salvador as well as the arrival of more Salvadoran troops led by the Vice Minister of Defense,

Francisco Adolfo Castillo. Before being able to land his helicopter, the ERP shot it out of the sky and captured him upon landing. The mission was a resounding victory for the ERP and by extension, the FMLN, which soon resulted in further legitimization of their movement in the eyes of potential aid donors from both the international aid community and from the Socialist Bloc countries, which provided more military aid thereafter via Nicaragua through the Gulf of Fonseca.

Several significant events took place in 1983. A barracks revolt on the part of Lt. Col. Sigfrido Ochoa at the Cabañas garrison temporarily paralyzed much of the military's operations until the matter was resolved. There was also a murder of a top level female FMLN guerrilla leader by the name of Melida Anay Montes in Nicaragua that symbolized deep schisms from within the insurgent ranks just as their numbers were swelling by the thousands. A new constitution was also signed after a year's worth of arguing. The pope also visited El Salvador with the blessing of the FMLN and the government, and the peace process began anew under the auspices of the Contadora treaties that took place on Contadora Island in Panama. Contadora called on the five Central American republics to end all fighting under certain conditions, which they all accepted, including Nicaragua. This action is what spurred the Reagan administration to pressure El Salvador, Costa Rica, and Honduras to withdraw their support, which they did. The peace process was then placed on hold for another year.

By 1984, the violence was still out of control, and larger numbers of people fled the country, became displaced internally, were conscripted into the military, or joined the guerrillas. The FMLN had grown to approximately 12,000 strong in a country of just five million. By comparison consider that this is the same size of the largest current day guerrilla organization in the Americas, the Revolutionary Armed Forces of Colombia (FARC) of Colombia, in a country of over 40 million, and the FARC continued to keep the government forces at bay there. The presidential election of March 1984 finally put Duarte into power, 12 years after his initial defeat and exile in 1972. However, the FMLN made one of their biggest mistakes in the process by sabotaging the election procedures on many fronts, which turned much of the population against them.

Although Duarte, a moderate by all standards, was president from 1984–1989, due to the ongoing war effort, his ideology did not rule the day. The forces of militancy driven by U.S. and right-wing policies in El Salvador instead were able to gain ground amid the supposed growth of democracy in the country. However, Duarte did accomplish some meager goals toward peace.

The most important among them in 1984 occurred in October and November, when he invited the FMLN to meet with his government ministers about moving toward peace. The problem with these talks was that both sides still represented diametrically opposed interests and the peace process stalled another three years. The elections of the following year for Legislative Assembly and municipal governments were swept by the Christian Democrats overwhelmingly due to a lull in the violence that year.

The reduction in violence was on both sides of the war. The FMLN reduced its numbers by half by 1987, and changed its tactics to calculate its strikes where they could most efficiently damage government interests without creating a wave of violence that would threaten the civilian population with massive government retribution as it had in the past. A major corruption ring was uncovered in an investigation in 1986 that implicated high level military officers who had received support from the United States, an act that could only have taken place under the move toward democracy, however limited it was, that was occurring under Duarte and the Christian Democrats.

By 1987, with so many measures exhausted to end the war, the new president of Costa Rica, Oscar Arias, came forward with a proposal that was soon widely accepted. In fact, he received the Nobel Peace Prize that year for his efforts, which came to fruition at the Esquipulas talks in Guatemala that year. Esquipulas opened up the peace process more than it resolved the crisis by putting into place several key peace-making staples. It brought the rebels and the Duarte government to the negotiating table in El Salvador; it brought UN troops to Central America in 1990–1991; and it brought the UN to observe elections in Nicaragua in 1990, among other stipulations. The Catholic and Lutheran churches also joined together in 1988 to discuss the future of the country and built a consensus opinion for peace.

The late 1980s signaled yet another sea change in El Salvador. The elections of 1988 spelled defeat for the Christian Democrats in the Legislature and victory for ARENA. Divisions were soon revealed within the Christian Democrats over who would run for president in 1989 just as Duarte came down with cancer. The outgoing president would finish his term but died in 1990. His party would have a difficult time removing the stigma produced from the corruption charges that cast doubt on the Christian Democrats' claims to represent honesty in public office. ARENA's candidate, Alfredo Cristiani won the presidential elections in 1989, beginning a wave of ARENA dominance of the presidency that continues to this day. The FMLN also began to change its tune during the election proceedings by providing their own analysis about the course the country should take, suggesting that elections be delayed for six months and offering to support the results and participate as well.

However, there were also ongoing atrocities that caught international headlines. In 1989, six Jesuits, their housekeeper and her daughter were brutally murdered by the Atlacatl Battalion. This incident triggered more investigations into past and present crimes against humanity perpetrated by the Salvadoran armed forces and it was discovered that most of the officers in charge of the massacre were former trainees of the School of the Americas, as was the case with the El Mozote massacre by the same unit in 1981, as well as the rape and murder of the four church women in 1980. The massacre of the Jesuits was the latest in a line of atrocities carried out by School of the Americas graduates that finally caused Maryknoll priest Roy Bourgeois to open SOAW in order to protest the school's existence in Fort Benning, Georgia.

In fact, Father Bourgeois had traveled to El Salvador earlier in the 1980s in order to spend time getting to understand the guerrillas and was targeted by the Salvadoran military as a result. He barely escaped the country with his life after Salvadoran officers boarded his return flight to the United States, demanding he come with them, when a TV news crew began filming the encounter, causing the officers to exit the plane. Father Bourgeois's organization draws tens of thousands of protesters every November to the gates of Fort Benning, Georgia on the same weekend in which the church women were killed, in honor of their loss and all the others who have died at the hands of the school's graduates. There is another side to the story, of course, which claims that the school can not be blamed for the atrocities of its students, and this debate has raged on in the U.S. Congress for over a decade as of this writing, with close to even splits in the chamber over whether or not to close the school down.

As the war appeared to wind down in 1989, George H. W. Bush (1989–1993) was inaugurated as the U.S. president. His administration was more inclined than the Reagan administration to include the guerrillas in peace talks while he continued apace with the same staunch U.S. support for the Salvadoran military effort. However, the U.S. Congress became less easy to convince of the necessity for funding the military after the murder of the Jesuits, and Bush had to work within stricter confines than Reagan did as a result. At the same time, the FMLN would surprise everyone with an attack in November that spread across the country and even to the capital, which was rare. After the 1989 guerrilla offensive, it was obvious that the over $4 billion dollars in U.S. aid to that point had not diminished the capacity of the FMLN. It had in fact created a larger civilian base of support, as can be seen by the continued viability of the FMLN after the war in the form of a legitimate political party. However, the power of ARENA, which was founded by death squad leaders, has also endured.

This political coexistence became possible in both cases due to the strength of the National Commission for the Consolidation of Peace (COPAZ) peace accords signed in January 1992 in Mexico City. The conditions for peace were several. The FMLN agreed to lay down its arms but wanted its members to be allowed to enter the National Civilian Police (PNC) force after giving up on a provision to enter the army, and they demanded the right to participate in the COPAZ peace process.

To end this chapter with a positive note, a review of the well-known story of Ciudad Segundo Montes. Segundo Montes, named after one of the slain Jesuits, was settled by former refugees who fled the violence of northern Morazán for the safety of Honduras in the early 1980s only to return to El Salvador and establish a new village in 1989. The camp in Honduras was known as Colomoncagua and it became internationally acclaimed for its relative self-sufficiency as well as for the camp community's ability to thrive under the leadership of war refugees. One of the revered leaders of Colomoncagua was the priest Miguel Ventura. Father Ventura was an ardent follower of Archbishop Romero's teachings and as a result of his stance against the military and in favor of the poor of Morazán, he was tortured by the military, and lived under a general threat to his life during the war.

His life represents the continuing legacy left behind by Oscar Romero, for Father Ventura's sermons to this day only mention religious doctrine to a limited degree, and instead focus almost exclusively on the socioeconomic and political problems that the Salvadoran people experience. His sermon from March 24, 2008 was largely a critique of neoliberalism as an abuse of the world's poor for the purposes of making the wealthy even wealthier, and he tied this analysis together with the political marginalization and criminal violence that the poor of El Salvador face each day. Romero spent his time struggling against state-sponsored violence against the poor, which was the principal problem they lived through in the 1980s, while Father Ventura and many other followers of Romero resist a new form of oppression from their perspective, which comes in the form of globalization. The next chapter discusses the postwar era in which issues such as this become the new arena of discussion for the nation.

NOTE

1. James R. Brockman, *Romero: A Life* (Maryknoll, NY: Orbis, 1989) 241, 242.

8

Reconstruction, 1992–2008

The 1992 Peace Accords made Salvadorans breathe a bit easier, for a moment, and then reality sunk in quickly and dramatically. Between 70,000 and 80,000 people had died, over one million people (one-fifth of the population) had been displaced, scattered to the winds across El Salvador, Honduras, Guatemala, Mexico, and the United States. Over 500,000 Salvadorans had fled to the United States alone, and most of them lived there without legal residency. The countryside was wracked with economic despair, littered with mass graves, and towns that were former shells of themselves. The ex-combatants and civilians wore their scars, too. Untold tens of thousands still carry their wounds, both inside and out. From the burns of the torture chambers to the malnourished children crying in the jungle night, it is impossible to separate El Salvador's past, however long ago it seems to us outside the country, from its present and future.

However, the war does not define the people. The country has made great progress toward rebuilding itself in the shadow of this horrific series of events. It must be remembered that El Salvador is not Rwanda, Sudan, or the Democratic Republic of the Congo, where genocides have taken the lives of seven million people since the end of the time of the Salvadoran war. This is merely to put El Salvador's conflict into perspective. In those conflicts, significant percentages of the population were eliminated; whereas in El Salvador, about

1.5 percent of the population was killed. However, the numbers are important because they quantify what is ultimately immeasurable, which is the extent of human suffering that the war caused. It is to the recovery efforts that we now discuss.

1993 TRUTH COMMISSION

One of the first steps toward recovery in most civil conflicts of the late twentieth century is truth commission to set the record straight about what occurred. El Salvador's truth commission was released in 1993 under the title "From Madness to Hope: The 12-Year War in El Salvador: Report of the Commission on the Truth for El Salvador." The report collected complaints of atrocities committed by both sides in the conflict, and found that just five percent of the complaints were against the guerrillas, thus demonstrating that the government's role in carrying out crimes against humanity was orders of magnitude higher than that of the resistance. The report does a good job acknowledging that both sides did indeed commit heinous acts, including abductions, torture, and executions of mayors, military personnel, and traitors by the guerrillas, and torture, abduction, and murder of wide swaths of the civilian and guerrilla population by the military and paramilitaries. However, there have been very limited amounts of judicial punishments meted out against the perpetrators of these crimes as part of the reconciliation process that has been necessary for the country to heal its wounds. This has been quite difficult in some ways due to the fact that the two dominant political parties since the war are composed of the very people and ideologies that were at each others' throats throughout the civil war.

There was no question that these sides would have to concede considerable amounts of ground in their ideologies in order for peace to sustain itself after National Commission for the Consolidation of Peace (COPAZ). The Farabundo Martí National Liberation Front (FMLN) had to concede to a free market economic system and the government had to concede to democracy. Unfortunately, terms such as free market and democracy often mean very little for the impoverished family hoping to be noticed by those residing in the capital, and their historical lack of trust in the institutions of government, given the history of that government, has recently led them to demand change, although without violence now.

For example, despite claims by government officials to be working toward change to alleviate poverty and inequality, land distribution was still so unequal in the years following the Peace Accords that landless peasants took matters into their own hands on October 23, 1995. Upward of 1,100 people decided to squat on lands in the west of the country that exceeded the constitutional limit of 245 hectares for private agricultural property. This sort of

grassroots activism became a more viable alternative for the average Salvadoran especially as a result of the organizing efforts of the liberation theology
wing of the church as well as former guerrilla groups, which had their roots
going back to the 1960s and 1970s. The state had long since proven itself incapable of responding to the needs of the majority of its citizenry in the eyes of
the common Salvadoran despite the 1992 accords ending the war and people
felt it necessary to take matters into their own hands as a result.

The 1980 Agrarian Reform law and a subsequent amendment set the stage
for this type of protest. The law was initiated under the governing junta as a
way of placating the rising tide of revolt in the countryside at the time, and
the hundreds of cooperatives that resulted from the expropriation of excess
private property did help alleviate poverty in some cases but it fell far short
of its goals. The limit of 245 hectares on private holdings had to be enforced in
order to have any lasting effect, however, and the landed elite, whose interests
ultimately paralleled the Nationalist Republican Alliance (ARENA) government's interests, were able to avoid the law through the mid-1990s. This was
the case despite the 1980s land reform program and the program designed to
help former government soldiers as well as former guerrillas and their supporters after the civil war called the Land Transfer Program (PTT). This last
program gave land to tens of thousands of families on both sides of the former
conflict but proved unable to solve the problem because of a lack of infrastructure to support these families in the future.

By 1994, landless peasants formed the Democratic Peasant Alliance (ADC)
to protest the continued holdings of over 245 hectares across the country.
Their cause was serious, as 83 percent of the farming population of the country was either landless or land poor by this time, signifying an increasing need
for land redistribution efforts in the minds of many people. The government
responded to the ADC's protests by dismissing their accusations, and thus
leaving the peasants with little options for appeal aside from nonviolent civil
disobedience in the form of squatting. Their actions met with some success,
increasing awareness of the problem, and an increase in support for the FMLN
political party in the rural and urban areas in and around places like Santa
Ana, the second largest city in the country, because it was the FMLN that provided financial support to these movements. Thus, the support the guerrillas
worked so hard to build from the 1970s on should be understood to have been
gained through grassroots organizing efforts and not the standard story from
the right-wing in El Salvador about a Moscow-led campaign to indoctrinate
Third World peasants around the world. If this were so, the two-way support
between the peasantry and the FMLN in the decades after the civil war would
have little reason for existence. It was the FMLN's ability to respond to the
concerns of the poor that made them a viable alternative to the centuries-old
system perpetuated by the military-oligarchy leadership. That is not to assert

that the FMLN has succeeded in their programs, or that the ARENA party is less able to create lasting change in the country. In fact, there are many poor Salvadorans to this day who deeply distrust the FMLN and instead support ARENA.

ELECTIONS OF 1994

The dominant political party since the end of the civil war has been ARENA, which was founded by Roberto D'Aubuisson among others, including the president from 1994–1999, Armando Calderon Sol. Calderon's background is in law, but he comes from a wealthy coffee-growing family and he also served as mayor of San Salvador and various other governmental posts before becoming president. Calderon is known for helping to incorporate the former guerrillas into public life, which is widely accepted as necessary. In fact, many former guerrillas have become respected members of national life in El Salvador due to the fact that the government under Calderon helped them acquire education and land after the war. On the other hand, he is also known for accelerating the country's path toward complete privatization and neoliberalism, which is deplored by the FMLN. The country experienced a period of democratic growth in these years, while also witnessing a rising crime rate. The nation's police force received massive amounts of training from the United States in order to professionalize its ranks, and El Salvador's law enforcement officials are generally more respected for this than their Latin American counterparts. Although corruption certainly occurs, Mexico and Guatemala have much worse problems still, with rampant problems associated with their police forces in the areas of drug trafficking, extortion, and so forth. The U.S. view of Calderon is that he should be praised for rebuilding the country after the civil war and that his efforts improved the economy considerably. The State Department views him as helping to turn the right-wing ARENA party into a legitimate political party by stabilizing the country.

The Salvadoran people themselves were divided over Calderon during his tenure. The president was still publicly loyal to the ideals of the founder of ARENA, Roberto D'Aubuisson, whom many viewed as the epitome of ultra-conservatism. This represented a tremendous source of fear for many Salvadorans who remembered the days of the death squads that D'Aubuisson was known to have supported, while the right-wing remained happy with the political situation. Others viewed Calderon's presidency as a more moderate version of the party's initial hard-line. The hard-liners celebrated the promotion of free trade policies that included the lowering of import tariffs and privatization, while the FMLN opposition led protests against these measures, which they viewed as detrimental to the jobs of the poor. Calderon felt the liberalization of trade was necessary in order to stimulate investment, and the FMLN criticized these moves as pandering to national and international elites. Calderon also came under heavy criticism after the UN issued a report demonstrating that death squads still operated throughout the country after the civil war with the participation of police and military elements. Calderon's efforts to punish these groups were seen by many as insufficient. Overall, his presidency was successful enough to get the next ARENA party candidate elected.

ELECTIONS OF 1999

The presidential elections of 1999 brought yet another ARENA candidate to power, perpetuating the overwhelming influence of the Salvadoran elite. President Francisco Flores (1999–2004) was the youngest head of state in North America at the time, and had an impressive political history for his age. He had previously served on the Legislative Assembly and had helped implement the plans of the peace accords of 1992, among other important tasks. He is especially criticized and simultaneously lauded for bringing El Salvador closer to the United States' sphere of influence. This connection of course has deep roots already, dating back to the nineteenth century, but it only increased through the years as ARENA politicians such as Flores viewed the United States as a necessary conduit of assistance on El Salvador's road to economic and political growth. President Flores also helped solidify the Central American Free Trade Agreement (CAFTA-DR) with the United States and the Dominican Republic, which received howls from the left and praise from the right. He even sent Salvadoran troops to Iraq in 2003, and although many troops remained as of early 2008, most were slated to return home soon. This was an unpopular move in Latin America as a whole, whose population was overwhelmingly against the U.S.-led invasion, and El Salvador's population was no exception. In fact, by 2008, El Salvador was the last Latin American nation to have troops left in Iraq. In a move to stabilize the economy even further that has changed El Salvador in still unforeseen ways, Flores switched El Salvador's currency from the *colon* to the U.S. dollar in 2001.

Reaction to Flores' policies have been mixed, as with the two past ARENA presidents. While dollarization was configured under the premise of preventing the problems associated with a currency of inferior value to the dollar, the use of U.S. dollars has led to inflation that many view as a detriment to the economy. At the same time, however, the economy has been improving considerably for many. For example, Metrocentro, the main mall in San Salvador, is the largest and most luxurious of all in Central America. Other examples include massive amounts of new home and hotel construction that has resulted both from increased exports in assembled goods and agriculture, as well as from tourism and remittances. All of this continued under Flores despite the ever-increasing problem of gang activity after the war, which has fundamentally decreased the public's trust in their government to protect them. Flores dubbed his anti-gang initiative as "la Mano Dura" or "the Firm Hand," which has not made a dent in the problem thus far, as the number of murders per year now reaches nearly 3,000.

ELECTIONS OF 2004

Flores's successor, Antonio Saca (2004–2009), was quite similar to his predecessor. Saca's background is rather different from the former presidents in several ways, however. He is the son of Palestinian immigrants (as was his FMLN party opponent, Shafik Handal) and his background is in sports journalism and business. Just after his 39th birthday, he defeated the much more seasoned FMLN candidate Shafik Handal, who was general secretary of the Salvadoran Communist Party (PCS) from 1973 to 1994, and was an FMLN guerrilla fighter beginning in the late 1970s. And while the presidential election was lost, the FMLN gained considerably more control within the Legislative Assembly during the midterm elections of 2006 with 32 seats versus ARENA's 34 seats. It is probably inevitable that the same rivalries that caused the civil war will continue within the political arena, but everyone involved prefers the unarmed struggle to the armed one of the past. CAFTA-DR (which officially includes the Dominican Republic) also officially took effect during Saca's presidency, in 2006.

Saca designed a similar plan to deal with the skyrocketing gang problem, naming it the "Super Firm Hand" after Flores's "Firm Hand." The plan increased police powers and spent more time and money on targeting gang activity, which is blamed for 60 percent of the murders in the country. This trend is continuing throughout Latin America, especially in countries such as Colombia, Mexico, and El Salvador, where the drug and crime problems go hand in hand. The governments plead for U.S. assistance, and they tend to receive it. However, as governments crack down, the violence on both sides always escalates. In some cases, as in Colombia, the violence recedes for a time, but in that case, the problems cross the borders into other countries. The problem of rising violence can be better understood within the context of the economic conditions. For example, we need to consider the fact that as of 2005, the top 10 percent of the Salvadoran population earned over 47 times more than the bottom 10 percent. When this fact is coupled with the knowledge that the gangs are made up of the poorest of the country's poor, then we understand that those being left out of the improving economic conditions have been driven to desperation, as occurs across the planet in similar situations. At the same time, land and housing prices are driven up due to the influx of U.S. dollars from Salvadorans working in the United States for better pay than those living in El Salvador, causing further tensions associated with income inequality.

ECONOMICS AND INTERNATIONAL RELATIONS

The economy changed dramatically because of the war as well. The economy has consistently grown since the cease fire under free market reforms, with reductions in poverty by over 50 percent from 1992 to 2006. The government also sought to diversify the economy by creating free trade zones, and by promoting tourism through infrastructure developments such as road improvements, increased security, and financial support for tourist-related businesses. The historically dominant elite controlled by the so-called fourteen families has experienced a shift in structure, so now many of those former coffee and sugar producing oligarchs have branched out into other businesses to adapt to the new globalization movement. Therefore, the connection between land and wealth no longer speaks generally of the country as El Salvador diversifies its economy. Ironically, these changes result directly from the neoliberal policies instituted by the very forces that used to represent the landed elite; that is, the ARENA party. Make no mistake, however, because ARENA is still the same conservative party bastion, but they have merely accommodated to the changes of the world market forces by diversifying the economy. At the same time, the country is advancing down a more progressive path economically due to the new elite's tendency to seek higher education in the United States and Europe. They are returning to their home country afterward to work for economic and political liberalism.

Tied into this diversification is the great demographic shift from the countryside to the cities, namely to San Salvador. Most of this took place during the war, when the rural areas were the primary target of the military and the capital was left more or less alone. With approximately several hundred deaths in the capital versus tens of thousands in the countryside, this is still significant to say the least. Still, the war zone atmosphere drove over a million people from their homes, tens of thousands of which fled to the cities to find work, and the result was a shift of 60 percent rural population before the war to 25 percent after the war. This has also been facilitated by the great outmigration of Salvadorans from the 1970s to the present, but which was mostly caused by the war. The remittances sent south from places like the United States and Mexico by Salvadorans amounted to four times the amount earned by the coffee export in 1998, indicating how dependent the population has become on this money. These remittances now reach three billion dollars per year from the United States to El Salvador alone. Farming still comprises a significant element of the rural economy as well. Although agriculture suffered tremendously during the war due to the fighting in the countryside, as well as from hurricanes and earthquakes in the past decade, it has come back with the rise in world market prices in sugar and coffee.

Trade has also facilitated increased international connections to El Salvador, particularly through free trade agreements. Countries within Central America, as well as Mexico and the United States are at the top of the list of allies, but the Dominican Republic, Chile, Panama, Taiwan, and Colombia also are important, and agreements with the European Union, the Caribbean, and Canada are also underway. The U.S.-Central America-Dominican Republic Free Trade Agreement (CAFTA-DR) is the foremost agreement that drives international trade connections at this time. Begun in 2006, CAFTA-DR expands El Salvador's access to the much-coveted U.S. market and provides for more manufacturing jobs in El Salvador. With the dollarization of the economy in 2001, El Salvador hoped to stabilize prices and the economy in general. The U.S. companies have also expanded their presence in El Salvador, with over 300 currently in the country. A recent development is the compact signed between El Salvador and the Millennium Challenge Corporation (MCC). The five-year, $461 million plan hopes to reduce poverty and increase incomes across the economy.

GUERRILLA TOURISM

There have been many efforts by the marginalized classes of Latin America to integrate themselves into the growing world economy, and El Salvador is no exception. In Panama, the indigenous Kuna peoples have utilized their *comarcas* (semi-autonomous communal land holdings) to preserve their environment and their culture while earning a living through tourism. Various Maya and Totonac groups have done the same across Mexico as well. These are combinations of ecotourism and cultural tourism that tend to attract socially and environmentally conscious tourists from the west. In El Salvador, the people of the department of Morazán have adopted a similar model but with a unique addition. While they promote ecotourism and cultural tourism they have added the element of guerilla tourism, so to speak. Many former guerrillas and their supporters formed the agency known as Prodetur, and have been managing a protected area known as the Rio Sapo Reserve where visitors camp out with the former guerrillas and receive guided tours of former battle sites, guerrilla encampments, massacre sites such as El Mozote, museums, and other zones of interest from the civil war. Prodetur receives aid from international organizations while keeping clear of corporations who would most certainly skim large amounts of money off the top of their profits. In this way, all of the profits are spread to the various businesses in the area in and around Perquin in particular, which lies just 8.5 miles from Rio Sapo.

Perhaps the most notable face around Rio Sapo is the tour guide, José Serafin Gomez. His story is indicative of how the guerrilla experience has transformed the lives of the generation that came of age in the 1980s. Serafin, as he calls himself, joined the guerrillas in 1981 at the age of 10 and quickly became adept at counterintelligence under the tutelage of a former Salvadoran military officer who understood the army's tactics. Serafin's first combat experience was at age 11, in 1982, and he continued fighting until the end of the war 10 years later. Like thousands of others, Serafin was robbed of both his adolescence and his ability to obtain a formal education. Even though he is extremely knowledgeable due to his real-world experience as a guerrilla, his ability to integrate back into society after having lived his formative years in combat was limited, and yet he responded proactively by helping to manage Prodetur in order to rebuild the economic base of northern Morazán. Serafin, like many other former guerrillas, bears no ill will toward most former soldiers, many of whom still live in the region. Mass murderers such as Domingo Monterrosa and Roberto D'Aubuisson are actually the exceptions in the minds of the former guerrillas and the military's other victims, and the average former soldier is seen as first and foremost a fellow countryman struggling to get by, as opposed to an enemy. This demonstrates the way in which people have moved past the war's hostilities, even as they are entrenched in the aftermath of the war's destruction.

WOMEN

The culture of El Salvador has obviously been shaped by events of the recent past to a large degree, and the role of women is an excellent example of this. For example, women made up 40 percent of the guerrilla combatant ranks and played an even bigger role in the area of clandestine support for the resistance effort. This inherently demonstrated the impossibility of maintaining the image of the subservient, weak woman and turned it on its head. Women were shown to be just as adept at fighting, tactics, and dying as their male counterparts, and this lent them a higher level of legitimacy at least among the guerrillas and their supporters, if not within the population as a whole. However, women also returned to the domestic sphere in large numbers after the war, indicating the entrenched influence of Latin American culture in spite of the advances in gender equality that occurred as a result of the war.

There have also been many more women in the status of *jefa de familia* or head of the household than ever before. This occurred especially after so many men were forced to flee the violence or were forced to join the armed services and the guerrillas, while women often had to remain behind with the children. Women's mobility is always compromised in wartime, wherever it may be, and they and their children were no exception in El Salvador. Something quite typical of Latin America in general that affects this is the existence of the informal economy in which people sell goods and services outside of an established, legitimate business, and women not only make up a majority of the workers in this area but 80 percent of those women are single mothers. The relatively recent addition of the maquiladora industry in El Salvador has had the same effect it has had in Mexico and neighboring Central American and Caribbean countries, which is a majority female workforce. In total, 60 percent of the heads of households in El Salvador are women.

Guerilla *Jefa de Casa*

An example of the Salvadoran *jefa de casa* is a woman with the guerrilla pseudonym "Leo." Leo lived in the Honduran refugee camp known as Colomoncagua as a child with her family as a result of the war in Morazán in the early 1980s. She went to school in Colomoncagua until she was 12 when she became inspired to join up with the guerrillas in El Salvador. She describes her motivation as childlike in the sense that the task seemed like a great adventure to her, even though she understood perfectly well the realities of life as a result of the horrors of the war. At 12, she became a highly competent field radio operator for both the General Command structure of the FMLN and for Radio Vencer-emos, spending five years fighting in the war in total. Toward the end of the war, "Leo" became pregnant with her first daughter, whose guerrilla father died in combat shortly thereafter. "Leo" had a second daughter, whose father did not acknowledge her, leaving "Leo" with two daughters to raise on her own. When asked about her predicament, she admits that life is hard, but she knows that her situation is not that uncommon in El Salvador.

CULTURE

Although El Salvador has so recently been through one of the worst civil wars Latin America has ever known, it is important to note that the people have not given up their spirit for life. Any population that has lived what they have lived must have this spirit in order to forge ahead. So this last section is dedicated to cultural areas of interest that reveal the character of the Salvadoran people. For example, there is an oral tradition alive and well in El Salvador where myths about mystical people and creatures that blend magic and realism into one, thrive. The Latin American literature genre of magic realism embodies just this type of storytelling that has become popular the world over.

The folklore told by Salvadorans today has its roots in pre-Columbian times when the Pipil, Lenca, Chorti, and others dominated the region. These tales indicate continuity with the rest of Latin America as well as their own Salvadoran values. The story of *La Cihuanaba* stands out as an example of ancient Mexican connections to the story of *La Llorona*, or the crying woman. In the Salvadoran case, *La Cihuanaba* has been condemned to a life as a grotesque monster for being unfaithful to her husband. Men who see her view an illusion of a beautiful woman who then becomes her real self and attacks them with ferocity and behaves in an insane manner. The possible morals of the story illustrate aspects of Salvadoran culture that reference works can not. El Salvador also has its own version of Robin Hood, named *el Partideño* (cattle driver). His story follows that he murdered a wealthy man for raping a woman and then spent his life fighting the rich on behalf of the poor. There is yet another parallel with Mexico here, for Pancho Villa (originally Doroteo Arango) began his fight against Mexico's elites after he killed a rich man for raping his sister.

Although El Salvador is not as well known for its literary traditions as its neighbors in Guatemala and Nicaragua due to the giants of those countries such as Miguel Angel Asturias and Ruben Dario, there are still many important Salvadoran authors. One of the most well known outside the country is a woman named Claribel Alegria, whose work has been translated and published many times on Latin American resistance history. Two impressive books are *They Won't Take Me Alive* (1983), about a woman guerrilla martyr in El Salvador, and *Death of Somoza* (with Darwin Flakoll, 1996), about the assassination of former Nicaraguan dictator Anastasio Somoza by Argentine guerrillas. These two are based on interviews with participants in the revolutionary struggles in Latin America, and they allow the reader to decide his own thoughts about these conflicts on his own through listening closely to the well-preserved voices and versions of those who lived them.

Salvadoran music in the wake of the revolution can help us understand how the civil war continues to shape the culture of the regions most affected by the fighting. Sebastián Torogoz fought and sang songs for the people of Morazán during the war. Sebastián's group, Los Torogoces de Morazán, served as an expression of the culture of the war from the perspective of the rebels and their supporters, as well as a source of motivation for the troops. Sebastián describes his role during the revolution as bitter sweet in a sense, because Los Torogoces would have to play for the rebels both after victories and after defeats, even after the band itself had returned from battle as armed insurgents. The music developed during the war told stories of fighting, love, tragedy, triumphs, community, and other aspects that resulted from an enhanced conception of the common Salvadoran's place in the nation as a whole. "Roxana," "Guerrero de Amor," "Batalla Comandante Gonzalo," and "La Guerrilla" are all songs about different aspects of life during the war that people across the country still listen to today, albeit especially in Morazán. Through music from people such as Sebastián Torogoces, Cutumay Camones, and others, the revolution lives on in people's memories, as a source of strength, community, and nostalgia.

Sebastián's personal story is also symbolic of the character, strength, intelligence, and beauty of the Salvadoran people. He was a young adult at the beginning of the war, and just like so many thousands of other Salvadorans, the military murdered his family, leaving him with little options. He chose to join the People's Revolutionary Army (ERP) guerrillas as a means to struggle for survival and change in his homeland. The ideals of communism and capitalism were the furthest things from his mind, according to him. All he knew was that his family had been eliminated, and that in order to survive, something had to be done, and the guerrillas provided an option for him. This dilemma was something that so many Salvadorans had to face, and often at their own peril, but at the very least they knew that the destruction surrounding them necessitated a response, whatever that meant. Sebastián now has a young daughter who represents a new direction in his life. He still sings to large or small crowds, and he works with the Prodetur tourism agency. His story represents what so many others have had to do in response to the repressive and divisive history of El Salvador. And he demonstrates that with a zest for life, including a great sense of humor, the people of El Salvador have the means with which to rebuild their society in the wake of such destruction. Sebastián sang many songs to a group of students and professors in March of 2008; among them was the following, which tells the story of the battle of Moscarron in 1982, but bears the title of a fallen guerrilla commander:

"The Battle of Comandante Gonzalo" by Los Torogoces de Morazán

To the north of heroic and very valiant Morazán
The Francisco Sanchez Front obtains great victories
Defeating battalions of Garcia's best
Trained by the Yanquis to finish off the guerrilla
The day of June 5 we initiated the campaign
Baptized with the name of Comandante Gonzalo
Hero of Usulután where he fell fighting and will forever
In the heart of the people
The campaign concluded with important victories
With the incredible capture of the vice minister of defense
Francisco Adolfo Castillo who now is a prisoner
Of the guerrilla forces even though Garcia doesn't like it.[1]

The English translation does the song less justice than it deserves, for when Sebastian sings it to crowds in Spanish, it conjures up memories of the war that range from sorrow to elation, and this is something that we as American observers could only imagine, but never truly understand. And yet, our presence was indicative of how the war internationalized El Salvador, and there were many other examples of this phenomenon, because thousands of visitors flowed into the country from across the hemisphere during the 1980s, and the effects of this have continued after the war. There were doctors, nurses, aid workers, military advisors, academics, journalists, and many other types of people who viewed the war within its global context. One such person that stands out is Venezuelan-born Carlos Henriquez Consalvi, the former head of Radio Venceremos, and current director of el Museo de la Palabra y la Imagen in San Salvador.

Consalvi was part of a growing group of Latin American journalists who felt that Latin American governments thwarted free speech, and therefore he decided to join the FMLN. Radio Venceremos became famous during the war because it was able to keep guerrillas and their followers both informed of the war's events and it boosted their moral. It also effectively demoralized the enemy. In fact, it was even instrumental in the assassination of Domingo Monterrosa. The Lt. Col. fell into a well-laid trap in which the guerrillas tricked him into believing he had captured the main radio receiver for Radio Venceremos, which was a decoy filled with explosives. Radio Venceremos participated by going off the air temporarily to foment the myth that its radio had been found. However, the guerrillas detonated the receiver in Monterrosa's helicopter soon after, killing him and his crew. During the war, the station grew in status because nothing like it existed in the guerrilla theaters throughout Latin America. After the war, Consalvi decided to open the Museo in order to create a place for Salvadoran historical study, complete with archival materials and several areas for exhibitions that rotate regularly. This is another example of how former guerrillas have been able to integrate into Salvadoran society, but it is more than that, because this form of integration provides linkages to the significance of the war and it provides a steady income for Consalvi and his employees. Seen this way, their knowledge of the war provides them with the ability to sustain themselves after the war, as well as to educate the public about its effects.

CONCLUSION

In conclusion, El Salvador's postwar era has experienced tremendous ups and downs. The benefits of the cease-fire to the civil war should not be underestimated. The ex-guerrillas claim that this is a result of their power to force the military to the bargaining table after their 1989 offensive demonstrated the extent of the FMLN's capacity to continue fighting. The military and ARENA assert that democracy resulted precisely because of their own efforts to defend the country from Communist terrorists. The nature of this debate is conflictive and will no doubt remain as such for the foreseeable future as long as both sides are so diametrically opposed to one another.

NOTE

1. Translated by the author.

List of Notable Historical Figures in El Salvador

Claribel Alegria (1924–). Although born in Nicaragua, she grew up in Santa Ana, El Salvador and then moved to the United States as an adult. She is a well-known modern author with a strong Salvadoran background, having written countless books, in addition to her social and political nonviolent resistance activism. Several of her books deal with revolutionary issues during the Cold War in Latin America. *They Won't Take Me Alive* (1983) is an account of a young Salvadoran guerrilla fighter's life and death during the civil war that allows the martyred revolutionary's friends and family speak for themselves in their representation of women in the Salvadoran guerrilla movement.

Pedro de Alvarado (1495–1541). Aside from being Hernán Cortez's right hand man in the conquest of Mexico in 1519–1521, Alvarado also conquered Guatemala in 1524 and El Salvador from 1524–1530. Known across Mexico and Central America for his extreme brutality, he is the first European villain of El Salvador's history.

Rufina Amaya (1943–2007). The sole survivor of the massacre that took place in the village of El Mozote in December of 1981. Rufina's husband and four children were murdered in the massacre along with 700–900 others in the immediate area. Rufina is the main reason why the story of the massacre reached the attention of the world due to her outspokenness in the face of a

U.S. administration that refused to acknowledge the military's actions and a repressive military apparatus. Today, Rufina is revered by the poor of El Salvador for her heroism in speaking out after the massacre.

Anastasio Aquino (1792–1833). Leader of the massive Los Nonualcos Indigenous uprising in central El Salvador in 1832–1833 in response to increased forced impressments of poor Indians into the military. He is executed in 1833 and soon becomes a martyr for the disenfranchised much like the rest of the heroes of El Salvador's poor throughout postindependence history. After his execution, his severed head was placed in a cage and put on display as a message to all other potential rebels.

Manuel Arce (1787–1847). Salvadoran by birth, Arce was the first president of the United Provinces of Central America in 1825.

Gerardo Barrios (1813–1865). A positivist militarist, Barrios is considered the favorite president of the Salvadoran military for increasing the role of the military in Salvadoran society. He was also a champion of the reunification of Central America, which provoked his arch rival, Guatemalan president Rafael Carrera, to invade El Salvador in 1863. He was overthrown in 1863 by his former ally, Francisco Dueñas.

Father Roy Bourgeois (1938–). A U.S. Maryknoll priest, Bourgeois is the founder of the School of the Americas Watch (SOAW). He began the organization as a protest movement against the U.S. Army School of the Americas (SOA) after the same Salvadoran army battalion from the infamous El Mozote massacre (Atlacatl) murdered six Jesuit priests, their housekeeper, and her daughter in San Salvador in 1989. Bourgeois's investigations found that many of the battalion's members had been trained at the U.S. Army School of the Americas. As a result, he opened SOAW in order to both call attention to U.S. foreign policy results in Latin America and to call for the closing of the school, which has trained over 60,000 Latin American military personnel since 1948. He is one of the primary links between U.S. and Latin American antiwar activism.

Salvador Carpio Cayetano (1919–1983). Former head of the Salvadoran Communist Party (PCS) who founded the first guerrilla group, the Popular Liberation Forces "Farabundo Martí" (FPL) in 1970.

Fernando Llort Choussy (1949–). El Salvador's most revered currently active artist for two reasons. First, Salvadorans and international visitors and artists alike appreciate his unique painting style that has often been described as childlike for its simplicity. Yet, this should not be mistaken for low quality, for the beauty and symmetry of Llort's work are beautiful by any definition of the word. Second, ever since Llort founded an artist's cooperative in the northwest mountain town of La Palma in the 1970s, his style of art is visible all over that town, making it a beacon to all art-loving and craft-loving visitors. Llort also maintains an art gallery in San Salvador to this day.

Roque Dalton (1935–1975). Perhaps the most well-known Salvadoran author, Dalton grew into a popular literary icon with a revolutionary fervor that eventually drove him to join with the People's Revolutionary Army (ERP). However, he soon became one of the country's most beloved martyrs after the ERP executed him over differences of opinion over the direction of the guerrilla movement.

Roberto D'Aubuisson (1944–1992). Known during the 1980s as the father of the death squads (La Mano Blanca) this former Colonel holds a number of other distinctions: he founded the ARENA political party that has dominated the presidency since 1989; he is responsible for orchestrating the assassination of Archbishop Oscar Romero; and he was ARENA's presidential candidate in 1984.

Father José Matías Delgado (1767–1832). One of El Salvador's most revered priests for his exemplary leadership within the church and for being the first president of El Salvador from 1821–1823.

José Napoleón Duarte (1925–1990). The leader of the first viable opposition movement against the military-oligarchy alliance since Farabundo Martí's aborted uprising in 1932. Duarte and the Christian Democratic Party (PDC) built a democratic movement between 1960 and 1972 that sought to overturn the decades-long institutionalization of military and oligarchical power in the country. During the election of 1972, Duarte's impending presidential victory was thwarted by the military government. Duarte subsequently supported a short-lived uprising and its failure led him to a self-imposed exile in Venezuela. He would return to El Salvador and eventually become president from 1984–1989.

Francisco Dueñas (1810–1884). After beginning his political career in the Legislative Assembly in 1837, he went on to serve three inconsecutive presidential terms (1851–1852, 1852–1854, 1863–1871), playing a tremendous role in conservative politics during the crucial years of liberal-conservative rivalry that took place after independence.

Rutilio Grande (1928–1977). Murdered in 1977 by a death squad, Father Grande was a liberation theologian and close friend to Oscar Romero. He is credited with being the primary inspiration for Archbishop Romero's activism. Romero had always been a friend to the oligarchy prior to Grande's murder, but with this act Romero became involved in the same form of nonviolent resistance that Grande practiced and preached. Grande's name is often invoked in the same breath as Romero's, and the archbishop kept a large photo of Grande in his living quarters up until his own assassination. The photo still hangs in the Oscar Romero Historic Center.

Juan Lindo (1790–1857). A Honduran by birth, Lindo was the first official president of El Salvador after 1841 independence from the rest of Central America. He served from 1841–1842, and later went on to be the president of Honduras from 1847–1852.

Miguel Marmol (1905–1993). Founder of the Salvadoran Communist Party (PCS).

Agustin Farabundo Martí (1893–1932). As opposed to his revolutionary counterpart and mentor in Nicaragua, Augusto César Sandino, this Salvadoran provoked a Communist-led uprising in El Salvador in 1932 that ended before it began due to Martí's capture, trial, and execution at the hands of General Maximiliano Hernandez Martinez. His Red Aid International inspired large numbers of Salvadorans from 1931–1932 and the movement was only cut short due to Martí's execution and the widespread and systematic massacre that General Martinez carried out that ended in the deaths of 10,000–30,000 people in 1932 *(La Matanza)*. Martí's legacy influenced the name of the umbrella revolutionary organization of the 1980–1992 civil war and continues in the name of the main left-wing political party of the country, also known as the FMLN.

Maximiliano Hernandez Martinez (1882–1966). This Salvadoran general is best known for orchestrating the 1932 event known simply as *La Matanza*. The general asserted that a communist uprising was about to take over the country in order to justify the rapid elimination of up to 30,000 people. He then went on to rule the country from 1932–1944, further entrenching the military as the central power of the country, in alignment with the interests of the oligarchy. He is one of El Salvador's villains, but only for the left wing. He is a hero of the military to this day, as can be seen in their Military History Museum.

José Francisco Morazán Quesada (1792–1842). Considered to be one of the great liberal politicians and military commanders of Central American history, Morazán was born in Honduras and led El Salvador from 1839–1840 in addition to being president of the United Provinces of Central America, Honduras, Guatemala, and Costa Rica throughout the 1830s and 1840s at various times. The department of Morazán, El Salvador is named after him.

Oscar Arnulfo Romero (1917–1980). This most beloved son of El Salvador is currently up for consideration by the Vatican for sainthood due to the

Salvadoran people's enormous outpouring of adoration for him both during his life and since his death. As the archbishop of San Salvador, Romero nonviolently resisted the government's repression against the largely unarmed poor population of the country. He called on the government to halt the repression and for this an unknown assailant assassinated him on March 24, 1980 while saying mass at the chapel of the Hospital of Divine Providence. It was later revealed that his assassination was orchestrated by death squad leader and future founder of the ARENA political party Colonel Roberto D'Aubuisson, also one of the country's villains. The people of El Salvador still celebrate Romero's life every year during the week of March 24 across the country.

Margarita del Carmen Brannon Vega (1899–1974). The most famous female Salvadoran poet, she is also known as Claudia Lars. She wrote and published poetry between 1934 and 1972.

Joaquin Villalobos (1951–). Head of the ERP, the largest guerrilla faction within the FMLN.

Rafael Zaldívar (1834–1903). This academic, physician, and liberal politician held the presidency for nine years (1876–1885) and is well known for marginalizing the *ejido* land system in the country for the purposes of export-led growth policies embodied by economic liberal philosophy.

Glossary of Selected Terms*

Achiote: Red seeds used for spice and food coloring

AD: Democratic Action

ADC: Democratic Peasant Alliance

Adelantados: Initial Spanish governors of conquered Salvadoran territory

Administrador: Administrator

AIFLD: American Institute for Free Labor Development

Alcaldes mayores: Municipal authorities

Archaic Period: This describes the period between 6000 B.C. and 2000 B.C. in which sedentary farming began

ARENA: Nationalist Republican Alliance

Atlacatl: Significant Salvadoran indigenous god, also the name of the elite Salvadoran military battalion responsible for the massacres at El Mozote in 1981 and of the six Jesuits in 1989

Atlatl: Implement with assisted mechanism for launching a spear

Atole: Nonalcoholic drink made from corn

---

* Includes acronyms.

Audiencia: Colonial term for a prescribed administrative unit as well as the high court system in the Spanish colonies

Ayuntamiento: Municipal council

Cabildo: City council

Cacao: Cocoa bean, used to make chocolate when combined with sugar

Cacique: Indian chief

CACM: Central American Common Market

CAFTA-DR: Central American Free Trade Agreement [Dominican Republic]

Calpullis: Equivalent to a clan, with chiefs who served as leaders, representatives, and advisors

Cédula de vecindad: State-issued identification card

Chocolatl: Sacred drink made from cacao beans and chilies

Chorti: Indigenous group located in western El Salvador and eastern Guatemala

COCA: Central American Workers Federation

Cochineal: Dye extracted from insect eggs

Comal: Griddle used to cook tortillas and pupusas

Comunidad: Community

Contras: Term used to describe the counterrevolutionary forces based in Honduras and Costa Rica that were supported by the Reagan administration in their efforts to oppose the Sandinista regime in Nicaragua

COPAZ: National Commission for the Consolidation of Peace

Corregidores: Colonial officials with authority over Indian communities

Creole: Spaniard born in the Americas

CRM: Revolutionary Coordination of the Masses

CRTC: Central American Revolutionary Workers Party

Cuscatlán: Pre-Columbian indigenous name for El Salvador

Cuscatlecos: Indigenous term for Salvadorans

Debt Peonage: Virtual enslavement of workers indebted to landowners

EGP: Guerrilla Army of the Poor

Ejidos: Communally held land

Encomenderos: Spaniards given control over groups of Indians with the responsibility of Christianizing them

Encomienda: Allotment of Indians to a Spaniard

ERP: People's Revolutionary Army

FAL: Armed Forces of Liberation

FALANGE: Anti-Communist Wars of Liberation Armed Forces

FAPU: United Popular Action Front

FARC: Revolutionary Armed Forces of Colombia

FARN: Armed Forces of National Resistance

Fefa de familia: Female head of household

Filibuster: Nineteenth century U.S. mercenary adventurers seeking to acquire Latin American territory

Finca: Farm

FMLN: Farabundo Martí National Liberation Front

FNOC: National Civic Orientation Front

The Fourteen Families: The group is known for having an unprecedented amount of financial and political control in El Salvador dating back to the nineteenth century. Also known as the oligarchy.

FPL: Popular Forces of Liberation-Farabundo Martí

FRTS: Regional Federation of Salvadoran Workers

FSLN or Sandinistas: Sandinista National Liberation Front

FUD: United Democratic Front

FUDI: United Independent Democratic Front

GDP: Gross Domestic Product

Guardia Nacional: National Guard, which served as the equivalent of the Army.

Hacendado: Owner of a great estate

Hacienda: Great estate

Indigo: Plant used for dying

ISTA: Salvadoran Institute of Agricultural Transformation

Itzcueye: The Pipil earth mother goddess

Jefa de familia: Head of the household

Jiquilite: Leaves that produce indigo

Junta: Meeting or group of leading government officials, often a label given to successful coup plotters once in government

Latifundista: Large landholder dedicated to food production

Lenca: Indigenous group located in eastern El Salvador

Lithic Period: This describes the period between 10,000 B.C. and 6000 B.C., predating the arrival of sedentary farming

Macana: Obsidian bladed weapons

Maras Salvatruchas: Main group of street gangs currently plaguing El Salvador's slums, also known as MS-13

Maya: This is the primary indigenous group that has inhabited the Yucatan Peninsula, Chiapas, Guatemala, Honduras, and parts of El Salvador since 500 B.C.

MCC: Millennium Challenge Corporation

Mestizo: Mixed race peoples, also known as ladino in Central America in particular

Milpa: A corn field in Mesoamerica

MNR: National Revolutionary Movement

Nahua: Ethnic and language designation given to the indigenous peoples of central Mexico who then spread to El Salvador through the Toltec invasions. As a result, the Pipil of El Salvador speak Nahuat, which is very similar to central Mexico's Nahuatl

OAS: Organization of American States

Obraje: Term used in El Salvador to refer to an indigo mill

Olmec: Term used to describe the parent culture of Mesoamerica that dominated the region from Mexico to El Salvador from approximately 1,800 B.C. to 400 B.C.

ORDEN: Democratic Nationalist Organization

PAE: Stability Adjustment Program

PAR: Renovating Action Party

Partido: Tax administrative section broken down by geographical regions in El Salvador

PCN: National Conciliation Party

PCS: Salvadoran Communist Party/Partido Comunista Salvadoreno

PDC: Christian Democratic Party

Peninsular: Spaniard born in Spain

Petates: Straw mats used for sleeping

Pipil: Indigenous group located in western El Salvador

PNC: National Civilian Police

Pokomam: Indigenous group located in western El Salvador

Pozole: Hominy soup

PPS: Salvadoran Popular Party

PRAM: April and May Revolutionary Party

Pre-Classic Period: This describes the lengthy period of development in El Salvador and greater Mesoamerica from 2,000 B.C. to 250 A.D. prior to the Classic Period

PRI: Institutional Revolutionary Party (Mexico)

Proclama: Political proclamation

PRTC: Central American Revolutionary Workers' Party

PRUD: Revolutionary Party of Democratic Unification

PTT: Land Transfer Program

PUD: Democratic Union Party

Pulque: Alcoholic drink from the maguey cactus

Pupusa: Traditional Salvadoran dish made from a thick corn tortilla containing cheese, pork, or other ingredients inside

PUSD: Unification Social Democratic Party

Quetzalcóatl: Important Nahua god of the feathered serpent

Remittances: Term for money sent from outside of El Salvador to El Salvador

Repartimiento: Colonially administered system of indigenous labor obligation

RN: National Resistance/Resistencia Nacional

SOA: The U.S. Army School of the Americas, formerly located in the Panama Canal Zone from 1948–1984, and located at Fort Benning, Georgia since 1984

SOAW: School of the Americas Watch

Socios: Assistants

Solar: Household garden in Mesoamerica

SRI: Red Aid International

Tamal: Known as a tamale in the United States, this Salvadoran dish is made from cornmeal and other ingredients such as chicken, beef, or pork

Tecti: Pipil term for lord

Terrateniente: Large landholder dedicated to coffee production

Tienda de Raya: Company store

Toltec: Group of indigenous peoples that spread their influence south from Mexico to Central America in the tenth, eleventh, and twelfth centuries, including El Salvador

Tortilla: Flat and thin or thick corn cake, used as a staple in Salvadoran cuisine

UCS: Salvadoran Communal Union

UDN: Nationalist Democratic Union

UNO: National Opposing Union

UPD: Democratic Party Union

Visitador: Colonial auditor/administrator sent by Crown authorities to the Spanish colonies

Vitalismo: Plan initiated by presidential candidate Arturo Araujo and his advisor, poet Alberto Masferrer that campaigned for safeguarding everyone's right to the minimum necessities of life in 1931

Zurrones: A 214 pound cube of indigo

Bibliographical Essay

For readers interested in books written in English on general Salvadoran history, the selection is slim, but you can refer to two excellent works in Alistair White's *El Salvador* (New York: Praeger, 1973); and David Browning's *El Salvador: Landscape and Society* (Oxford: Oxford University Press, 1971). Most of the books written on El Salvador tend to concentrate on the era of the civil war and those texts do include a lot of good general history information as well. Tommy Sue Montgomery's *Revolution in El Salvador: From Civil Strife to Civil Peace* (Boulder, CO: Westview Press, 1995) is perhaps the most well known of this genre. There are also a plethora of sources dealing with U.S. involvement in El Salvador and in Central America in general, most of which I highly recommend. Walter LaFeber's *Inevitable Revolutions: The United States in Central America* (New York: Norton, 1993) is a very accessible history of U.S. foreign policy in Central America going back to the mid-nineteenth century. There are also a variety of personal accounts that would be of great interest to readers, notable among them is Charles Clements's *Witness to War: An American Doctor in El Salvador* (New York: Bantam Books, 1984).

Students interested in finding more general information such as that found in chapter one can go to the *CIA World Factbook* on El Salvador, found online at https://www.cia.gov/library/publications/the-world-factbook/geos/es. html. This site contains up-to-date facts on El Salvador including detailed information on geography, government, economy, and communications. The U.S. State Department's Human Rights Country Report on El Salvador also serves as a good site for the status of crime, the economy, and safety in the country right now. Several encyclopedias helped to fill in some of the details on El Salvador's regions. William LeoGrande and Carla Anne Robbins's article, "Oligarchs and Officers: The Crisis in El Salvador," (*Foreign Affairs* 58, No. 5, 1084–1103), reflects the growing interest of American foreign policy specialists in El Salvador at the time. Two important points should be noted here. One, most scholarly books and articles about U.S.-Salvadoran relations have been published after the civil war began in 1980 and two, LeoGrande himself wrote perhaps the most in-depth book on the United States in El Salvador during the civil war (which includes a large section on Nicaragua as well), called *Our Own Backyard: The United States in Central America, 1977–1992* (Chapel Hill: University of North Carolina Press, 1998).

Readers interested in the pre-Columbian and Conquest history of El Salvador have a variety of texts to consult. Murdo MacLeod's lengthy study of the Conquest and colonization of Central America titled, *Spanish Central America: A Socioeconomic History, 1520–1720* (Berkeley: University of California Press, 1973) provides good insights into El Salvador as well as the rest of the region. For those interested in the Maya influence in El Salvador, read the sections on El Salvador in Michael D. Coe's overview of the Classic and Post-Classic Maya, titled *The Maya* (New York: Thames and Hudson, 1999). Students seeking to comprehend the Pipil Indians should read William Fowler Jr.'s *The Cultural Evolution of Ancient Nahua Civilizations: The Pipil-Nicarao of Central America* (Norman: University of Oklahoma Press, 1989). Robert Sharer's always monumental and consistently updated study on the Maya titled, *The Ancient Maya* (Stanford, CA: Stanford University Press, 1994) gives some small bits of information on ancient El Salvador as well.

There are also a number of materials that are dedicated exclusively to the archeology of pre-Columbian El Salvador, including Robert Sharer's edited volume titled *The Prehistory of Chalchuapa, El Salvador* (Philadelphia: University of Pennsylvania, 1978) and works by the eminent specialist on ancient El Salvador, Payton Sheets. Sheets has led the way in Salvadoran archeology for over two decades with excavations culminating in works such as "The Prehistory of El Salvador," in *The Archeology of Lower Central America*, edited by Frederick W. Lange and Doris Z. Stone (Albuquerque: University of New Mexico Press, 1984); and he has at least two edited anthologies, titled, *Before the Volcano Erupted: The Ancient Ceren Village in Central America* (Austin: University of Texas Press, 2002); and *Archeology and Volcanism in Central America: the Zapotitlán Valley of El Salvador* (Austin: University of Texas Press, 1983).

Other authors have also tackled the pre-Columbian Salvadoran world, such as Arthur A. Demarest, whose work in the highland community of Santa

Leticia produced *The Archeology of Santa Leticia and the Rise of Maya Civilization.* Lewis C. Messenger Jr. looks at El Salvador as a frontier area before the arrival of the conquistadors in his "Community Organization of the Late Classic Southern Periphery of Mesoamerica: 'Expressions of Affinity?'" found in *Interaction on the Southeast Mesoamerican Frontier: Prehistoric and Historic Honduras and El Salvador,* Part II, edited by Eugenia J. Robinson (Oxford: British Archaeological Reports, 1987). Students looking for information on the cultural continuity of Salvadoran indigenous communities are well to look into *Indian Crafts of Guatemala and El Salvador,* by Lilly de Jongh Osborne (Norman: University of Oklahoma, 1975). Other studies of ancient El Salvador include *Cihuatan: an Early Postclassic Town of El Salvador . . . the 1977–1978 Excavations,* by Karen Olsen Bruhns (Columbia, MO: University of Missouri-Columbia, 1980); and E. Wyllys Andrews V's *The Archeology of Quelepa, El Salvador* (New Orleans: Middle American Research Institute, Tulane University Press, 1976).

Chapter three draws on a number of important sources about the colonial period that students can find quite easily. Jordana Dym's "'Our Pueblos, Fractions with No Central Unity:' Municipal Sovereignty in Central America, 1808–1821," (*Hispanic American Historical Review,* August 2006, 86:3, 431–466) examines how El Salvador and other Central American colonies faced the difficulty of nationalist cohesion during the move toward independence afterward due to their long history of a municipality focused concentration of power. Those students interested in the interplay between the Spanish government in El Salvador and the economic realm there should read works such as Robert W. Patch's chapter titled, "Commerce, Colonialism, and Corruption in Central America," found in *Latin America and the World Economy,* edited by Richard J. Salvucci (Lexington, MA: D.C. Heath and Company, 1996, 12–20); Miles L. Wortman, *Government and Society in Central America, 1680–1840* (New York: Columbia University, 1982); Hector Lindo-Fuentes's *Weak Foundations: The Economy of El Salvador in the Nineteenth Century* (Berkeley: University of California Press, 1990); David Browning, *El Salvador: Landscape and Society* (Oxford: Oxford University Press, 1971); and Murdo J. MacLeod's *Spanish Central America: A Socioeconomic History, 1520–1720* (Berkeley: University of California Press, 1973).

Chapters four and five focus on the century after independence from Spain, and readers looking for solid sources on this era will find a small number dedicated exclusively to El Salvador. The best I have found are Alistair White's *El Salvador* (New York: Praeger, 1973); Hector Lindo Fuentes' *Weak Foundations* and his chapter, "El Salvador from Indigo to Coffee," in Salvucci's edited volume (Berkeley: University of California Press, 1990, 68–78); and the Salvadoran government's official website on Salvadoran presidential history titled, "Casa Presidencial, El Salvador," http://www.casapres.gob.sv/gobernantes/fmarin.htm. Students with an interest in the Matanza and its aftermath (chapter six) can consult a number of high-quality books such as *Matanza* by Thomas Anderson (Lincoln: University of Nebraska Press, 1971); the website of "Casa Presidencial, El Salvador"; Alistair White's *El Salvador* (New York: Praeger, 1973); Jeffrey M. Paige's *Coffee and Power* (Cambridge, MA: Harvard University Press, 1997); Walter LaFeber's *Inevitable Revolutions* (New York: Norton, 1993); Stephen Webre, *Jose Napoleon Duarte and the Christian Democratic Party in Salvadoran Politics, 1960–1972* (Baton Rouge: Louisiana State University Press, 1979); and William Stanley, *The Protection Racket State: Elite Politics, Military Extortion, and Civil War in El Salvador* (Philadelphia, PA: Temple University Press, 1996).

Chapter seven focuses on the road to civil war and the war itself. The main source readers should consult is Tommie Sue Montgomery, *Revolution in El Salvador: From Civil Strife to Civil Peace* (Boulder, CO: Westview Press, 1995). This work does the best job in illustrating both the roots of the revolt and the roots of the military repression during the war. Other works that can supplement our knowledge of this conflict include Mark Danner, *The Massacre at El Mozote: A Parable for the Cold War* (New York: Vintage, 1994); Stephen Webre, *Jose Napoleon Duarte and the Christian Democratic Party in Salvadoran Politics, 1960–1972* (Baton Rouge: Louisiana State University Press, 1979); Charles Clements, *Witness to War: An American Doctor in El Salvador* (New York: Bantam Books, 1984); William LeoGrande, *Our Own Backyard: The United States in Central America, 1977–1992* (Chapel Hill: University of North Carolina Press, 1998); James R. Brockman, *Romero: A Life* (Maryknoll, NY: Orbis Books, 1989); and James Hodge and Linda Cooper, *Disturbing the Peace: The Story of Father Roy Bourgeois and the Movement to Close the School of the Americas* (Maryknoll, NY: Orbis Books, 2004). I also gained tremendous insight through interviews and conversations with former guerrillas and citizens of the departments of Morazán and Chalatenango in the north of the country. Chapter eight relies on the small number of sources that have become available since the end of the civil war, but students with an interest in the rebuilding of Salvadoran society should nonetheless read *Landscapes of Struggle: Politics, Society, and Community in El Salvador,* edited by Aldo Lauria-Santiago and Leigh Binford (Pittsburgh: University of Pittsburgh Press, 2004); newspaper articles from *La Prensa Grafica* in El Salvador; the Federation of American Scientist's Congressional Research Service, http://www.fas.org/irp/crs/index/html; the U.S. State Department's website, http://www.state.gov; and as with myself, the former guerrillas of Morazán and Chalatenango are available for first-hand accounts through the agency of Prodetur, which operates out of Perquin.

Index

About the Author

CHRISTOPHER M. WHITE is Assistant Professor of History at Marshall University.